The Development of Western Civilization

Narrative Essays in the History of Our Tradition from
Its Origins in Ancient Israel and Greece to the Present

Edited by Edward W. Fox
Professor of Modern European History
Cornell University

THE EMERGENCE OF ROME

As Ruler of the Western World

BY CHESTER G. STARR, JR.

THE EMERGENCE OF

ROME

As Ruler of the Western World

CHESTER G. STARR, JR.

Second Edition

GREENWOOD PRESS, PUBLISHERS
WESTPORT, CONNECTICUT

Library of Congress Cataloging in Publication Data

Starr, Chester G., 1914-
 The emergence of Rome as ruler of the Western World.

 (The Development of Western civilization)
 Includes index.
 1. Rome--History. I. Title. II. Series.
DG209.S73 1982   937   82-2939
ISBN 0-313-23561-9 (lib. bdg.)   AACR2

Second Edition 1953.
Seventh printing, with revisions, 1965.

Reprinted with the permission of Cornell University Press.

Reprinted in 1982 by Greenwood Press,
A division of Congressional Information Service, Inc.
88 Post Road West, Westport, Connecticut 06881

Printed in the United States of America

10 9 8 7 6 5 4 3 2 1

Foreword

THE proposition that each generation must rewrite history is more widely quoted than practiced. In the field of college texts on western civilization, the conventional accounts have been revised, and sources and supplementary materials have been developed; but it is too long a time since the basic narrative has been rewritten to meet the rapidly changing needs of new college generations. In the mid-twentieth century such an account must be brief, well written, and based on unquestioned scholarship and must assume almost no previous historical knowledge on the part of the reader. It must provide a coherent analysis of the development of western civilization and its basic values. It must, in short, constitute a systematic introduction to the collective memory of that tradition which we are being asked to defend. This series of narrative essays was undertaken in an effort to provide such a text for an introductory history survey course and is being published in the present form in the belief that the requirements of that one course reflected a need that is coming to be widely recognized.

Now that the classic languages, the Bible, the great historical novels, even most non-American history, have dropped out of the normal college preparatory program, it is imperative that a text in the history of European civilization be fully self-explanatory. This means not only that it must begin at the beginning, with the origins of our civilization in ancient Israel and Greece, but that it must introduce every name or event that takes an integral place in the account and ruthlessly delete all others no matter how firmly imbedded in historical protocol. Only thus simplified and complete will the narrative present a sufficiently clear outline of those major trends and developments that have led from the beginning of our recorded time to the most pressing of our current problems. This simplification, however, need not involve intellectual dilution or evasion. On the contrary, it can effectively raise rather than lower the level of presentation. It is on this assumption that the present series has been based, and each contributor has been urged to write for a mature and literate audience. It is hoped, therefore, that the essays may also prove profitable and rewarding to readers outside the college classroom.

The plan of the first part of the series is to sketch, in related essays, the narrative of our history from its origins to the eve of the French Revolution; each is to be written by a recognized scholar and is designed to serve as the basic reading for one week in a semester course. The developments of the nineteenth and twentieth centuries will be covered in a succeeding series which will provide the same quantity of reading material for each week of the second semester. This scale of presentation has been adopted in the conviction that any understanding of the central problem of the preservation of the integrity and dignity of the individual human being depends first on an examination of the origins of our tradition in the politics and philosophy of the ancient Greeks and the religion of the ancient Hebrews and then on a relatively more detailed knowledge of its recent development within our industrial urban society.

The decision to devote equal space to twenty-five centuries and to a century and a half was based on analogy with the human memory. Those events most remote tend to be remembered in least detail but often with a sense of clarity and perspective that is absent in more recent and more crowded recollections. If the roots of our tradition must be identified, their relation to the present must be carefully developed. The nearer the narrative approaches contemporary times, the more difficult and complicated this becomes. Recent experience must be worked over more carefully and in more detail if it is to contribute effectively to an understanding of the contemporary world.

It may be objected that the series attempts too much. The attempt is being made, however, on the assumption that any historical development should be susceptible of meaningful treatment on any scale and in the realization that a very large proportion of today's college students do not have more time to invest in this part of their education. The practical alternative appears to lie between some attempt to create a new brief account of the history of our tradition and the abandonment of any serious effort to communicate the essence of that tradition to all but a handful of our students. It is the conviction of everyone contributing to this series that the second alternative must not be accepted by default.

In a series covering such a vast sweep of time, few scholars would find themselves thoroughly at home in the fields covered by more than one or two of the essays. This means, in practice, that almost every essay should be written by a different author. In spite of apparent drawbacks, this procedure promises real advantages. Each contributor will be in a position to set higher standards of accuracy and insight in an essay encompassing a major portion of the field of his life's work than could ordinarily be expected in surveys of some ten or twenty centuries. The inevitable discontinuity of style and interpretation could be modified by editorial co-ordination; but it was felt that some discontinuity was in itself desirable. No illusion is more easily acquired by the student in an elementary course, or is more prejudicial to the efficacy of such a course, than that a single smoothly articulated text represents the very substance of history itself. If the shift from author to author, week by week, raises difficulties for the beginning student, they are difficulties that will not so much impede his progress as contribute to his growth.

Grateful acknowledgment of aid and encouragement in the development of this series is due to the contributors and to Mr. M. L. W. Laistner.

This essay, *The Emergence of Rome as Ruler of the Western World*, by Mr. Chester G. Starr, Jr., the first of the series to be published, was carefully revised for the second edition. It provides an account—unique in English in its brevity, clarity, and comprehension—of a period of European history which, for all its significance for our tradition, has ceased to constitute a ponderable part of our intellectual cargo.

EDWARD WHITING FOX

Ithaca, New York
September, 1956

Contents

Prologue ~~~~~~~~~~~~~~~~~~~~~~

IN A.D. 144 a Greek orator traveled from Asia Minor to Rome and there delivered in Greek a famous oration in praise of Rome. Among other remarks, he asserted to the Romans that "all the civilized world [i.e., the Mediterranean] raises with one voice the prayer that your Empire may endure in eternity." The name of this orator, Aelius Aristides, was half-Greek, half-Latin.

Such a person must appear remarkable to anyone who has ever looked at the Greeks of the classic period with their haughty division of the world between "Greek" and "barbarian," their narrow city-state loyalties, their dislike of autocracy. To explain how a Greek of the second century after Christ could express such ideas, we must consider the emergence into civilization of the power which he praised so highly, the Roman Empire. Particularly significant in the story are the creation by Rome of a political and military machinery with which it could conquer the Mediterranean, the effects of that conquest upon Rome, and the fusion of Roman culture with Greek civilization. The resulting urban, Mediterranean civilization which throve after the establishment of the celebrated "Roman peace" forms a summation of ancient civilization on which all later ages have directly built.

CHAPTER I

Geography and Peoples
of Ancient Italy

ITALY occupies the central position in the Mediterranean. It is otherwise favored by nature to such an extent that in modern times it has been the only purely Mediterranean state to claim the title of "great power." Essentially Italy is a long, narrow peninsula running south-southeast from the European continent, 650 miles in length and varying between 100 and 150 miles in width. On the east it looks across the cold, stormy Adriatic to the abrupt coasts of modern Yugoslavia and Albania; on the west its shores are bathed by the gentle Tyrrhenian Sea, which stretches west and south to the islands of Corsica, Sardinia, and Sicily.

Geographically Italy is divided into two almost equal, but quite dissimilar, regions. One is peninsular Italy, which is a typically Mediterranean land; the other is the area to the north drained by the Po River and its associated streams. This continental Italy partakes of the characteristics of the European continent, from which it is separated by the mighty sweep of the Alps. In medieval and modern times the north has led in Italian development; in the ancient world areas closer to the major Mediterranean center of civilization were more progressive.

The main mountain chain in Italy is that of the Apennines. Thrown up in relatively recent geological times, these limestone mountains still have sharp outlines but do not rise above 10,000 feet. From the vicinity of Genoa the Apennines march almost straight east to the Adriatic, thus separating peninsular and continental Italy. They then hug the east coast, so leaving the rich volcanic lands of Etruria, Latium, and Campania to the west, but below Naples they cut back across the peninsula to the west coast and follow it southwards until they jump across to Sicily. The plains in southern Italy lie on the east coast, in dry, dusty Apulia. But one must not overemphasize the word "plains"—in Italy the hills are everywhere, sometimes connected in ridges which eventually lead back to the Apennines, sometimes rising by themselves, but all serving to divide the arable land into small sections. People live in clusters in Italy, often in stone villages which cling to the hillsides to gain a certain source of water, to avoid the rush of armies in the lowlands, and to spare the all-too-scarce good land for farming.

The climate of Italy is that of the Mediterranean generally, though modified somewhat to Italy's advantage. During the winter the peninsula lies within the zone of the westerly winds, which bring rain in sudden storms. South of the Apennines the winter cold is tempered both by the warm Mediterranean Sea and by a good deal of sunshine—Rome is on the latitude of New York but enjoys the temperature range of the North Carolina coast. In the spring the westerlies begin their annual shift north away from the Mediterranean. In their place the Saharan blast furnace attracts from the European continent a rather steady northeast wind, devoid of rain. So sets in the summer drought; the rivers, recently in flood with the winter rains, dry up; and the fields turn brown under the dazzling sun. The rainless months in Italy, however, are fewer than in Greece or Palestine. Sicily has four months without rain; Rome, usually less than two; and the Po Valley, which never entirely loses the rain-bringing westerlies, can also count on melting snow from the Alps to feed its rivers throughout the summer.

The Dominance of Agriculture

Italian terrain and climate alike tend to favor agriculture over industry and commerce. The limestone mountains covering much of Italy are almost devoid of minerals, which appear chiefly in the older crystalline layers of Etruria. Here early settlers mined copper and lead, and offshore in the island of Elba they found the chief source of Italian iron. These deposits probably were enough to satisfy the simpler economy of the ancient world, but tin and the precious metals in any quantity seem always to have been lacking. The general absence of navigable rivers and the regularity of the Italian coastline, which is particularly pronounced along the Adriatic, did not favor commerce. Some ports, however, were available on the southern and western shores by which trade with the more civilized eastern Mediterranean could be conducted.

Although Italy thus had some trade and some basis for industry, it was celebrated in antiquity chiefly for its forests, pastures, and fields. The Apennines seem to have been heavily timbered at the dawn of history; the Tiber, for instance, was long a logging stream, down which floated the cuttings of the central mountains. Since the ancients were as prodigal with their forests as modern man, the wooded areas of Italy constantly shrank, and by the time of Christ the more accessible slopes had been cleared. The devastation was assisted by the ubiquitous goats, who ate off the seedlings. Once the rocky slopes lost their cover entirely, the soil washed quickly away, and today the slopes in heavily settled areas are bare or support only bushy growth.

The chief animals raised on Italian pastures were sheep and goats, because they were small, easily moved, and tolerant in diet. Since lowland pastures tended to dry up in the summer drought, grazing involved an annual cycle of movement, especially after the Romans had conquered all peninsular Italy. During the winter the animals lived in the lowlands, chiefly of Apulia; then, as summer came on, they were driven up into the mountains of central Italy along regular paths which are still in use today. Large herds of cattle and horses were to be found only where good pastures could be assured the year around, as along the coast or in the Po Valley; still they were more common in Italy than in the eastern Mediterranean. The term Italia itself means "calf-land."

Agriculture was the chief pursuit in historic times, but its rhythm was (and is) quite different from that which we know in the United States. In the first place, the Mediterranean climate dictates a concentration of most crops in the rainy season from autumn through spring. The Italian farmer planted his barley or wheat in the fall (from September on) so that it could germinate with the fall rains, live through the relatively mild winter, and come to maturity with the spring rains for a harvest in May or June. Grapes and olives, both very important in the farmer's economy, were harvested in the fall, but were so long-rooted that they did not need irrigation through the summer drought.

Again, ancient agriculture required careful, intensive work. Usually one-half of a farmer's field would be left fallow each year to regain its fertility. Agricultural experts advised that while fallow it be plowed three or even four times, in addition to manuring. Since the plow was light and had no colter, furrows were neither deep nor well broken; as the husband drove the oxen, the wife and children followed along behind the plow, breaking up the clods with hoes and other simple instruments. The fact that farms often were only two or three acres in size is more understandable when one considers the great amount of human effort required to extort food from the soil. As we follow Roman development, it is worth remembering that the men who made the history of Rome were trained in the hard life of the farm and that farming always remained their chief occupation. The rhythm of the agricultural year underlies the history of Italy.

To sum up the effects of geography on that history, one may say that Italy is primarily an agricultural area, which can support a relatively large population. In climate and terrain it is definitely Mediterranean, though its northern edge shades into continental European; northern Italy has frequently had invaders from across the Alps, while southern Italy has as often been invaded from the south or east. Farther from the seats of Oriental civilization than Greece, Italy would naturally be slower to pick up the developing culture of the eastern Mediterranean, but its southern and western coasts had receptive harbors for the foreign traders when they began to come west. Italy is well fitted to be the leader in a unified Mediterranean, but the peninsula itself is not easily to be united merely because it is marked off by seas and the Alps. On the contrary its hills and mountains tend to divide it sharply, and influences from without have often pulled it apart. The Roman achievement in uniting its numerous peoples was a great one.

Early Peoples

The "dawn of history" came in Italy about 700 B.C. By this date a great deal had happened in Italy as well as in the rest of the Mediterranean world. Though Italy itself was thus far a backward area, it had passed through the Paleolithic and Neolithic ages, and was at 700 in an iron-age civilization. As a result of invasion by peoples from every possible direction, its population was a variegated mixture of four main stocks.

Two of these groups came during prehistoric times. The first was a Mediterranean-type people whom the gradual desiccation of the Sahara drove north from Africa about 5000 B.C. Short-limbed, long-headed, dark in skin, this stock furnished the physical base for the Italian people henceforth. In the main the African invaders were shepherds in a low level of Neolithic civilization. From the east they gradually picked up the use of copper and bronze, especially in south Italy and Sicily.

The second wave began moving about 2000 B.C. from the northeast across the eastern Alps, where there are broad, easy passes less than 3,000 feet in height. This wave, which spoke Indo-European dialects, was connected with parallel movements about the same time into Persia, Asia Minor (Hittites), and Greece. To Italy this element contributed the future language stock and also a great deal of its basic culture, for the invaders settled in villages and lived by agriculture. It appears that various echelons of people speaking Indo-European tongues came into Italy in the second millennium.

By 1000 iron had been introduced into Italy from an iron-using center in the Hungarian plain.

By 700 the first two peoples, those of Mediterranean type and those speaking Indo-European tongues, had merged and formed an agricultural civilization resting on the use of iron for tools and weapons. To take Latium as an example, the farmers lived together in villages, frequently but not universally perched in a defensible position above the Latin plain. Several villages formed a canton, and the Latin cantons felt a common bond, expressed chiefly in common religious ceremonies; but they might and did fight with each other. Within the villages the family was a remarkably strong social unit under the control of the father. Living in a world where his very existence depended on the forces of nature, a Latin farmer was deeply religious in an animistic sense, i.e., he believed that the world was full of spirits embodying the forces of nature that must be propitiated. At his death he would be cremated and his ashes buried in an urn shaped like his hut with high, thatched roof. While life essentially was much the same anywhere in Italy at this time, local differences in culture loomed large. In most parts of Italy the local dialects resembled Greek. This can be seen in the word *pur* meaning "fire," which has survived today in our word "pyromaniac." In Latium, however, the dialect which later became Latin most resembled the Lithuanian and Slavic tongues. In these *ignis*—as in our "igneous"—was the word for "fire." Linguistically, politically, and culturally Italy started in diversity.

The remaining two stocks arrived at the dawn of history. Both the Etruscans and the Greeks came to Italy from the eastern Mediterranean and carried in their ships and minds much of the far more advanced civilization of that area.

Among other skills came the art of writing, so that truly historical material about early Italy begins to appear after 700. Once contact had been fully established between Italy and the East, it was never thereafter broken. The intensity of the connection varied from time to time but tended ever to increase; eventually the master of Italy was to turn to the east and conquer the area from which the peninsula had been civilized.

The Etruscans

The first of these two eastern peoples, the Etruscans, is, for the historian, one of the most puzzling and exasperating groups in the ancient world. It now appears that they came from Asia Minor about 850 B.C. Perhaps they were drawn by the mineral riches of Etruria; perhaps they were spurred by troubles at home. Probably we should visualize their movement as one of small groups, swooping down on the coast north of the Tiber, easily moving inland over the rolling ground of Etruria, then settling down in a chosen area as a governing minority. Their rapid conquest was facilitated by superior technique in war and by their closer social organization. Each group, as it established itself in an area, built a walled, hilltop city and fashioned about it a city-state, usually under a king or war-leader who later gave way to an aristocracy. Although twelve of the Etruscan states assembled in a religious union, they remained politically independent and rarely co-operated.

The Etruscans would be important if they had done no more than introduce into Italy the idea of the city-state; for, as the experience of Greece proves, the city-state form of organization released great social and political powers in ancient man. Rome eventually became such a state through imitation of the Etruscan model and thereby started on its great path of expansion. The Etruscans, however, did much more for central Italy: they introduced many aspects of eastern Mediterranean civilization and at the same time took over a great deal from the native iron-age culture. Rarely original, they deftly combined elements from everywhere into a pleasure-loving civilization which baffled alike intellectual Greek and sober Roman.

Very largely they borrowed from the Greeks. Thus they took over the Greek alphabet before 700, altered it somewhat to fit their language, and passed it on to Rome; thanks to the Etruscans our alphabet today is short in vowels and redundant in the C, K, and Q group. Like the Greek, Etruscan sculpture emphasized the human in a naturalistic sense. In architecture and in all the arts Greek motifs and styles were usually dominant. The tombs of Etruria are so filled with vases from the great period of Athenian pottery that such vases were long known as "Etruscan."

Yet one is not long in feeling that despite their wide borrowing the Etruscans were unique in the ancient world. Their aim, to quote a sympathetic modern, was "the enjoyment of a fair existence and the delights it can offer." So they took what the world had to offer, but adapted it in rich, local variations. Their tombs were often decorated with gaily painted frescoes, depicting banquets or the like; in one early case the wall is a seascape where ducks and other birds flit about, dolphins jump out of the water, and men dive in from a steep rock. In the bulging muscles of Etruscan terra-cotta sculpture one senses the same realism and earthiness as in the low, earth-clinging temples of the Etruscan cities. The Romans could never understand or admire the Etruscans, and in that antipathy one can learn a great deal about the character of both sides.

Politically the power of the Etruscans in Italy was both extensive and brief. After the easy conquest of Etruria independent bands swarmed north across the Apennines into the Po Valley in the sixth century. Even before this they had moved south, about 650, to Capua in Campania, proceeding by land and taking a good deal of Latium and also Rome in the process. By the beginning of the fifth century their power was falling as rapidly as it had risen, but in the meantime the Etruscans had done much to civilize central Italy.

The Greeks

Their southward expansion brought the Etruscans into direct contact with the Greek settlements in Italy. The resulting hostility goes far to explain the Etruscan decline. When the Greeks began to press out of the Aegean Sea in all directions after 800 B.C., the most favored area for settlement was south Italy and Sicily. This Greater Greece could easily be reached by a coasting voyage up the west coast of Greece to Corcyra and a short trip across the mouth of the Adriatic to the heel of Italy. Not only was the climate of the new area much like that of Greece, but also a number of good ports tempted the Greeks to explore the timber, wheat fields, and other resources of the western lands.

Greek settlement of Italy was largely a haphazard process in which various strains of the homeland were jumbled together, but each settlement or "colony" constituted an absolutely independent city-state. The Greek settlements stretched from Cumae on the Campanian coast, important in early Roman history, down the west coast and along the instep past Sybaris to Tarentum. In Sicily the Greeks took over the eastern two-thirds of the island; here Syracuse eventually became the most important state. Nor, though it is outside Italy, may one overlook Massilia (Marseilles) in southern France, which pushed its outposts down into Spain; for Massiliote ambitions and fears were often a pregnant force in Roman affairs. In all major particulars the civilization in these city-states was a part of general Hellenic culture. These western states had magnificent ambitions and built on a vaster scale than parent Greece, but their architecture, like their sculpture and thought, was on Greek lines.

Like the Etruscans and the Phoenicians in Africa, Sicily, and Spain the Greeks were expanding territorially in the sixth century. The result was a series of wars of great significance. At first the Etruscans and the Carthaginians, who now controlled the Phoenician settlements, united against the Greeks and stopped their expansion into Corsica and southern Spain. Then the allies went each his own way, with most disastrous results. The Carthaginians were defeated at Himera in Sicily in 480 and were so prevented from throwing the Greeks out of Sicily. The victor, Syracuse, joined Cumae in opposing the Etruscans on the sea in 474; we still have an Etruscan helmet which the ruler of Syracuse dedicated in triumph at Delphi.

The result of these wars was to ensure that no one foreign power was to be dominant in Italy. The Carthaginians were to continue to control western Sicily, Africa, and most of Spain until Rome crushed them in the Punic Wars; the Etruscans were to hold central Italy in a loose, more and more inert grip until the Romans were ready to take it over; the Greeks, potentially most powerful of the three, tore each other to pieces in interstate rivalry and eventually fell almost thankfully into Rome's hands. Their gallant fight against the other two had made it clear that the lasting foreign influence in Italy was to be Greek. Unconsciously the Greeks had protected Rome in its early days, and they were eventually to lead her into her first overseas expansion. In 500, however, it should be noted that Greek civilization, though vigorous, had not yet reached its great heights of the Periclean Age.

After the close of the wars of the sixth century most of Italy was still politically independent, though the Indo-European peoples occupying it were steadily more influenced by cultural currents from the East. The question now was: Which of the local peoples was to be the one to conquer the peninsula, if indeed any were to carry out the difficult task of unifying the whole of Italy?

CHAPTER II

The Rise of Rome in Italy ～～～～

THE largest river on the western coast of Italy is the Tiber, which in antiquity was a natural artery of trade both for foreign goods and for the salt obtained at its mouth. The key position along the stream lay at a point 15 miles inland. Here an island in the Tiber marked the end of navigation for ancient seagoing vessels and also afforded an easy crossing for the north-south trade route along the coast. The low land of the coast yields at this point to hillocks, some rising in isolation close to the river, others running out from the plateau toward the stream. This strategic position was the site of Rome.

The City-State of Rome

The hills of Rome seem to have borne scattered villages from 1000 B.C. On the Palatine, overlooking the Tiber island, lived Latins; and on the other hills lived Sabines from the central mountains. These villages apparently united in a religious league; and then, shortly before 600 B.C., they took the decisive step of coming together in a city-state ruled by a king. A sewer (*cloaca maxima*) was built to drain the swamp below the Palatine and the reclaimed area became the market, the *forum*, of the new city. Rome was now in existence.

The formation of a city-state at Rome reflects the development of trade in the area. It was also spurred by imitation and perhaps fear of the Etruscan cities to the north; by 600 B.C., at any rate, the Etruscans themselves held possession of Rome as a way station on their route to Campania. Under the leadership of Etruscan kings Rome became the dominant state in Latium and annexed a considerable area along the Tiber. To match its new magnificence a great temple was built on the Capitoline Hill, copying Etruscan styles but dedicated to the Italic deities Jupiter, Juno, and Minerva, who were represented by terra-cotta statues. Though temple and statues alike were originally alien ideas to the Roman mind, this temple eventually became the center of Roman faith. In later days the consuls were to make their solemn vows for the safety of the Roman state each year at the temple of "Jupiter Best and Greatest"; and triumphing generals, dressed in the purple of the old kings, were to mount the Capitoline in their chariots to deposit their wreaths of glory.

About 500 B.C. the power of the Etruscans began to wane in central Italy. One result was the expulsion of the Etruscan kings at Rome by the local aristocracy, who established an oligarchical republic in which the highest magistrates were two consuls, elected for one year. The Etruscans had given Rome a tremendous cultural impetus and in its political power a memory of greatness to which it could look back, but the cultural pattern of the area remained basically Indo-European. After the expulsion of the kings the Roman aristocrats lost control over their Latin neighbors and were forced to accept a permanent defensive alliance against the hillsmen, in which Romans and Latins were equal. About this same time a cultural unit existing along the Tiber Valley broke up, and Greek imports ceased. Together with central Italy Rome slipped into obscurity as the fifth century—the age of Pericles in Greece—began.

The Early Romans

The history of Rome from 500 to 265 B.C. may be summed up briefly as consisting first of a dark century, in which the city barely held its own, and then of a period of increasing light as Rome conquered Italy after 400 B.C. To the later Romans their earlier history was interesting chiefly as an illustration of Roman character. Their greatest historian, Livy (T. Livius, 59 B.C.–A.D. 17), displayed an intense patriotism as well as the usual moral sensitivity of an ancient historian when he claimed in his preface:

Either love of the task I have set myself deceives me, or no state was ever greater, none more righteous or richer in good examples, none ever was where avarice and luxury came into the social order so late, or where humble means and thrift were so highly esteemed and so long held in honor.[1]

If we are to understand the significance of Roman history and the reasons for the expansion of Rome, it is worth stopping a moment to investigate this Roman character, as revealed in traditions and in religious beliefs. The traditions, which were preserved mainly in the family and so passed from father to son for generations, were often tied intimately with landmarks about the city; points such as the Tarpeian Rock, the Lake of Curtius, the Sister's Beam, and others— each had its tale pointing some patriotic virtue. Together, these traditions reveal a patriotic people who were above all

[1] Except as otherwise noted, this and subsequent quotations are from the translations in the Loeb Classical Library (by permission of Harvard University Press).

else obedient to established, legal authority—the family, the state, and the gods.

The Roman family was a very tightly knit unit under the father, whose power (*patria potestas*) over his offspring was almost unlimited. Not only did he hold legal title to all property of his sons, but also he might sell them into slavery or even put them to death for misbehavior. Toward the state the Romans showed their obedience in their respect for law, their deference to the more experienced citizens who had "authority" (*auctoritas*), and their scrupulous regard for the traditions of their ancestors (*mos maiorum*). Though Roman ways changed, they did so slowly.

Toward the gods the Romans were devout in both the family and the state; Cicero proudly called them "the most religious of mortals" from early times. Though the rise of commerce and industry under the kings had brought the introduction of Greek deities and the beginnings of Greek ideas of worship, the early religious calendar was still almost entirely Roman. Essentially the gods were viewed as dis-embodied spirits or powers, which could be won over by the right prayers and sacrifices; their will was revealed in the flight of birds and in thunder. The primitive ideas of magic were largely excised through aristocratic influence within the state religion, which was highly precise and formal; if the state did its duty to the gods, it hoped that the gods would be pleased and co-operative. If so, then Rome enjoyed "peace with the gods" and prospered; if not, things went awry, and the duly appointed officers had to restore the peace by sacrifice and extraordinary vows of temples or other honors. The individual had almost no place in this worship; the magistrates of state, assisted by religious ex-perts, did everything for him, and on religious days the private citizen needed only to keep quiet. In its aristocratic control, centralization under state guidance, simplicity, and sense of order Roman religion is perhaps our best mirror of conditions in the early Republic.

The Romans of this period appear also in tradition as hard workers, earning their livelihood from the soil and defending their gains against the savage hillsmen. Romans were always proud of telling the story of Cincinnatus, called from the plow to head the army against an invasion, defeating the enemy, and then returning to his plow. Such a life possessed what the Romans called *gravitas*—essentially a serious, public-spirited outlook on life, which was not calculated to encourage arts and letters. The emphasis on the group in religion, state, and society tended to limit individuality; it is late in the Republic before true individuals appear in the history of Rome.

Much of what the later Romans tell us about their forebears is clearly patriotic exaggeration or misinterpretation. Myths are easily built up and last long. Still, the modern historian has come to suspect that they often conceal a kernel of truth. And so, as one considers the characteristics of the early Romans, one can see that they are in large part real attributes of a simple, conservative, agricultural society resting on a long tradition of family life. Beset by enemies on all sides, this society had to fight hard and continuously; it is not accidental that *virtus* to a Roman meant pre-eminently military prowess. Such a people might have its defects in matters theoretical; on the other hand, it had the great advantages of practical adaptation to real life and a sense of law and discipline to serve as a stiffening fiber. To explain Roman success we must come back again and again to the

Romans themselves, and as Rome expanded we must look for the inevitable, but difficult, changes in their character.

The Roman Conquest of Italy

Serious, hard-working, the Roman faced the world, confident in his gods, and they did not fail him. During the years 500–265 B.C. the Roman state extended its control to all of peninsular Italy. At the same time it became a democracy. These internal and external changes are inextricably intertwined: the expansion abroad required general co-operation and unity at home and at the same time softened internal problems by giving foreign outlets; the internal changes were made possible only because the military needs of the state forced the aristocrats to give way to the commoners at crucial points. It is a pity that the whole process is so little known; rarely in history has a state been able to carry out such great changes without violent explosions or conflict between external and internal policies.

The expansion itself, when taken up as briefly as it must be here, may lead to the impression that Rome had a "manifest destiny" driving it from success to success, but a closer study would show that Rome made many false starts and retreats during the two hundred-odd years required for the conquest of Italy. The conquest itself falls into two phases. Down to 350 B.C. Roman armies operated in a small area on the western side of the Apennines. In the fifth century Rome and the Latins barely held their own against the thieving, covetous hillsmen, but gradually the plainsmen beat back their opponents. Shortly after 400 Rome captured and destroyed the nearest Etruscan city, Veii, only to fall victim itself in 387 to an irruption of wild Gauls from north Italy.

The Roman army was defeated, Rome was sacked and burned, and the Gauls left only after the payment of an indemnity.

Buildings had suffered, but the people remained; by 350 Rome had regained its lost prestige and power. The base now established, Rome proceeded in the next eighty-five years to conquer all Italy south of the Po Valley in a series of stubborn wars. In general the Romans won by dividing their enemies both politically and geographically, i.e., gaining alliances with some possible foes against others, and carving up actual opponents by driving wedges through their territories. In these wars the Roman armies were greatly improved by a reorganization which made the basic infantry unit, the legion, an articulated group of smaller units (maniples) which could fight in the mountains as well as the plains; the generals, however, remained the yearly changing consuls.

As they advanced, the Romans opened up roads along strategic routes and established colonies of Roman and Latin families as permanent garrisons at key points. Land hunger certainly must not be discounted as a reason for the expansion of Rome; it has been estimated that conquered states on the average lost one-third of their land for the benefit of Roman settlers. Otherwise the defeated were not unduly penalized. They yielded control of their foreign affairs, they entered a permanent alliance with Rome by which they agreed to furnish a set number of men to the Roman army, but they paid no taxes and retained autonomy in their local affairs.

On the whole Rome showed remarkable liberality, at least after the Gallic invasion, and varied its policy to fit the local conditions. Particularly impressive was Rome's willingness to grant its own citizenship to subject states after they had proved their loyalty. The states of Italy were much less fully developed than the cities Athens had tried to dragoon into its Aegean empire, and so fell more easily into Rome's system; but the Roman liberality must also be given credit for helping to solve the problem of uniting conquered states under one ruler. The sensible, practical, tenacious character of the Romans goes far toward explaining not only the initial conquest but also the relatively easy acceptance of their rule.

Internal Development

The problems of internal government were essentially two. In the first place, the expanding territories occupied by Roman citizens required an ever more extensive machinery of government; secondly, within Rome itself there was a long-continued struggle between the aristocrats and the other classes for control of the political system. When the aristocrats, called patricians, led the revolution about 500 B.C. which expelled the kings, they set up a government consisting of three parts. The chief magistrates were two consuls, elected from the patricians for one year; these republican safeguards of choosing officials for only one year and of dividing one post among several persons remained the normal characteristics of all magistracies added thereafter. The Senate was a body of experienced men chosen by the consuls for life, which technically gave only advice but actually spoke for the patricians as a whole. The assembly, which had limited powers, was organized in a peculiar fashion: the people were divided into thirty wards or *curiae*, and within each ward the majority carried the vote of the whole ward. The patricians, with their retainers, were usually able to control this Curiate Assembly: voting was not secret, discussion was allowed only if the consuls called on a specific person for his opinion, and the assembly could vote solely on matters put by the consuls. Since the patricians also controlled the priesthoods, which were the fount of law, it is apparent that they had a tight control over the government at the beginning of the Republic.

The commons, called plebeians, were in the majority but were at the outset divided. Some were fairly well to do or small, independent farmers; others were traders, living largely on the Aventine Hill at the southern edge of the city; others yet, called clients, were economically dependent on individual patricians and so were obligated to support them in any altercations. As a whole the plebeians had no voice in the government. Their civil rights were limited by the patrician control of the courts and by such rules as an early ban on intermarriage between patrician and plebeian; economically they were often in debt—and at this time debts were secured by a pledge of one's own freedom. If a plebeian could not repay the grain he had borrowed, he and his family might find themselves slaves.

The only advantage on the plebeians' side was the fact that Rome of the fifth century was threatened on all frontiers; if it was to survive, the plebeians must be willing to fight for the state. As Rome began later to expand, the plebeians became ever more important. The result was a slow retreat of the patricians from their privileged position without the necessity of revolution. Though the story of that retreat is one devoid of historic personalities, it is nonetheless a dramatic unfolding of a remarkable series of events, one of the most interesting constitutional developments in recorded history and one revealing the political sagacity of the Roman people.

Early in the fifth century the plebeians took a remarkable step. If they might not have a voice in the government, they would form their own extralegal agencies of government. The result was the gradual evolution of a purely plebeian assembly called the Tribal Assembly, headed by ten annually elected tribunes with two aediles to supervise the plebeian treasury on the Aventine. In the assembly the plebeians could formulate their grievances and draw up resolutions (plebiscites); then, under the leadership of the tribunes, they poured out and enforced their decisions. The tribunes were authorized to aid their fellow plebeians in questions of taxes and conscription, and from this function eventually derived a general power of veto over the act of any magistrate of the state.

Such a system was a serious threat to the regular system of government. The patricians, however, could do little beyond protesting its illegality, for the plebeians backed their assembly and their leaders with the threat of overwhelming force or of secession from Rome. Since the patricians could not hope to continue without the plebeians, they usually, but reluctantly, had to give way. One effort seems to have been made in the middle of the fifth century to get rid of the entire system of Tribal Assembly and tribunes by admitting plebeians to the regular magistracies and so giving them adequate protection. This effort was connected with the writing down of the law in the famous Twelve Tables (about 443–442), which had been demanded by the plebeians. The Twelve Tables were accepted and became the earliest monument of Roman jurisprudence, but the accompanying effort to reform the government was rejected by the patricians. Thereafter the Tribal Assembly and the tribunes with their obstructive veto continued on past the end of the Republic. Always a danger to the regular workings of the state, the plebeian machinery was usually limited by the practical sense of the Romans; the tribunes, for example, had no power over consuls or other magistrates while outside Rome on military expeditions.

The next step in the advance of the plebeians occurred in the late fifth century, when the Roman army was reorganized as a phalanx of heavily armored infantry. Since more men were needed, the wealthier plebeians were conscripted as well as the patricians, and the army was grouped into centuries (hundreds) of different classes on the basis of the amount of equipment each class could afford. As this army, organized in centuries, came together each spring at the Field of Mars outside Rome, the custom arose of having it decide various matters connected with the campaign by voting in centuries. At some unknown point this army organization turned into a true assembly, the Centuriate, which replaced for all practical purposes the old Curiate Assembly. The significance of the shift lies in the fact that now people were classed by wealth rather than birth—Rome was now a plutocracy rather than an aristocracy.

During the fourth century the plebeians finally made their way into the regular offices of state, ending with the right of admission to the major priesthoods in 300 B.C. The Tribal Assembly essentially became an organ of the state, and in 287 the Senate was constrained to give up its power to reject plebiscites after the assembly had passed them. This date is usually taken as the point at which Rome technically became a democracy.

The richer plebeians, to be sure, had been the ones to gain the most in the battle, and were soon to coalesce with the patricians to form the aristocratic class of the later Republic.

The poorer farmers had no chance to rise to public office, which was unsalaried. Their condition, however, had improved to some extent through the economic benefits of conquest, and one hears less of famine and debt at Rome in the third century than in the fifth. One leader of the conservatives, Appius Claudius the Censor, had tried in his censorship (about 312 B.C.) to uplift particularly the plebeians living in the city proper and the sons of freedmen, perhaps with the hope that he could attract their support to the patricians against the richer plebeians; but his efforts, reminiscent of similar efforts by Bismarck and Disraeli, were out of time and were erased by almost universal consent. Appius Claudius, incidentally, is one of the first Romans to loom up out of the mist as a real individual. Builder of the famous Appian Way to the south and of the first aqueduct into Rome, he was thoroughly hated by many of his fellows, who ascribed his blindness in old age to the wrath of the gods. His last great act was to be carried into the Senate to deliver a fiery oration against King Pyrrhus, a Greek adventurer active in southern Italy from 280 B.C. on. This oration, written down and published, was one of the first landmarks in Roman literature.

The Developed Roman Constitution

By 287 B.C. the Roman constitution was much changed and enlarged from that of the early Republic. In theory the people ruled, and there was complete civic and political equality. Speaking through the Tribal or Centuriate Assemblies, as the occasion demanded, the people elected their magistrates and passed laws as they desired. The voice of the people, however, was not without restriction. Both assemblies were formed on the ward principle (35 tribes,

193 centuries), and in both the presiding officer—tribune or consul—held tight control over oratory and the proposal of measures. Only in Rome could one vote, so that many of the Roman citizens, scattered now over central Italy, were in essence disfranchised.

The assemblies, moreover, met infrequently; but Rome controlled so vast an area that problems were always arising. The day-to-day business and the execution of the people's decisions were the affair of the Senate and the elected magistrates. The Senate by this time consisted of about 300 senior statesmen of Rome, usually ex-magistrates, chosen for life by the censors (see below). Its function was still primarily that of advice, but it exercised wide control over Rome's subject states, directing the preparation of treaties and supervising their observance. It also controlled the finances of the state, and as a permanent body had a pervasive influence on many aspects of government. To a Greek ambassador of the third century, impressed by its collective sagacity and responsibility, the Senate was "an assembly of kings."

Each year the citizens regularly elected thirty-one magistrates to run their affairs for the coming year. Ten of these were judges in cases where a person's freedom was questioned, and ten were tribunes. The other eleven are more significant. At the top were the two consuls, with equal powers, who gave their names to the year. In the city they usually alternated in actual office; in the field each usually took a separate army and operated in a different zone. If, however, both were together and could not agree, then the state machinery came to a halt. To get around this impasse it was possible for the Senate to appoint one person as dictator for six months with overriding powers, and dictators appeared in cases of emergency down to the end of the third century.

Below the consuls was the praetor, whose early history is much argued. By this time he was becoming the officer in charge of the judicial system, and more praetors were added later as that system grew more extensive. Next were the four quaestors, or financial officials; and last were the four aediles, who supervised the roads and markets of the city itself. Once each five years the Romans also elected two censors, who arranged the citizen body according to wealth for the purposes of taxation, conscription, and position in the Centuriate Assembly, filled vacant seats in the Senate, and stigmatized unworthy citizens. One ex-consul, we are told, was removed from the Senate in 275 for having more than ten pounds of silver-plated dishes. The censors also let state contracts for roads and the maintenance of public property.

Rome in 287 had essentially a city-state form of government, expanded somewhat to take care of the problems of empire but still quite simple. No official existed to oversee education, health, sanitation, or the like; all these matters were managed within the individual family by the father, who also kept his sons and slaves in order. Again, outside Rome most problems of government were handled by the subject states, and only major problems of interstate rivalry or common defense came before the Senate and the consuls for decision. The system was one of decentralization and simplicity—a strength at this time, but later a nearly fatal weakness.

The Roman Citizenry in 265

In almost all respects the Roman world was still a simple one after the conquest of Italy. Rome itself was a backward, overgrown town. Around it lay the holdings of the dogged, simple Roman farmers who aroused amusement and yet awe in the Greeks they were now meeting. Literature, art, and philosophy were almost unknown. Our sources gravely inform us that the first barber appeared in central Italy in 300 B.C., coming from Sicily; the first divorce of record had not yet occurred by 265. Thus far the Romans had shown themselves gifted not in culture but in political and military organization.

Nevertheless there were signs, especially in the religious field, that the citizenry was already by 265 no longer content to be treated as one great, disciplined mass. Throughout the conquest of Italy the Romans had carried out their religious rites and felt they had thereby gained victory. The result, however, was an increasing sterility in the Roman religion and a slow discovery that it did not quite fit the needs of the people. To fill the gap the priests turned to Greek rites, and from the siege of Veii one finds Greek religious ritual and Greek gods, with their more plastic, appealing character, trickling into the city. Processions, sacred banquets, games of different sorts suggest that the Romans felt a need for individual participation in the religious rites.

If individualism was gradually appearing as Rome grew great, then one might expect some interesting reactions in the rest of the third century. In this period Roman soldiers first set foot outside the Roman peninsula, and the Roman people met the full impact of Hellenistic civilization. The effect upon an already shifting Roman character might well be explosive—and so it was.

CHAPTER III

Rome Conquers the Mediterranean

DURING the period 264–133 B.C. Rome strode out of the Italian peninsula into the Mediterranean world like an all-conquering colossus. First it took the western half of the Mediterranean basin; then, after 200, its armies turned eastward into Greece and Asia. Geographically such an expansion of a unified Italy may have been inevitable; but certainly the political and cultural conditions then existing in the Mediterranean aided the process. Politically the area was divided into many mutually hostile states and so invited conquest; culturally it was becoming ever more one unit, that embraced by Hellenistic civilization. The entrance of Rome into this world resembles the introduction of a magnetic field. All the particles which before drifted about aimlessly swung together in patterns centering on Rome; moreover, while lines of force radiated out from Rome, strong countercurrents of Hellenistic civilization flowed in upon it.

The Hellenistic world, at which we must look briefly, represents an absorbing part of the development of ancient civilization. Originating in the Macedonian conquest of the Orient under Alexander (334–323), it was in many respects a very modern world. Socially cosmopolitan, its life was one of large cities. The political relations among its states

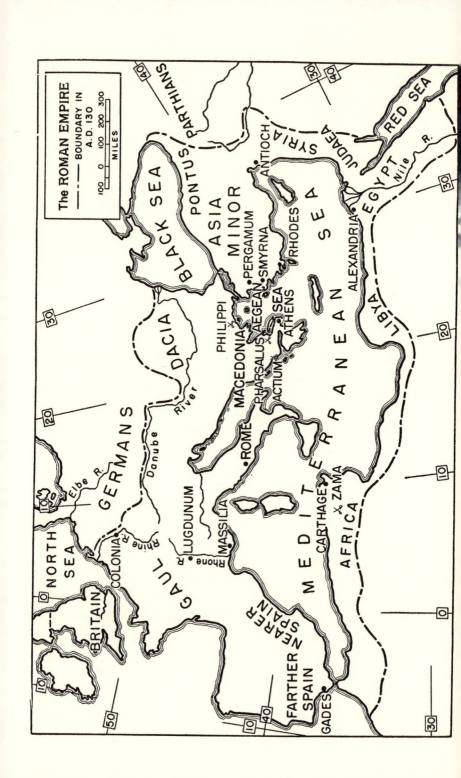

The ROMAN EMPIRE
—— BOUNDARY IN
A.D. 130

100 0 100 200 300
MILES

NORTH SEA

BRITAIN

GERMANS

GAUL

Elbe R.

Rhine R.

COLONIA

LUGDUNUM

Rhone R.

MASSILIA

NEARER SPAIN

FARTHER SPAIN

GADES

AFRICA

CARTHAGE

ZAMA

MEDITERRANEAN SEA

ROME

Danube River

DACIA

BLACK SEA

PONTUS

PARTHIANS

ASIA MINOR

PERGAMUM

SMYRNA

RHODES

ANTIOCH

SYRIA

JUDEA

EGYPT

Nile R.

ALEXANDRIA

LIBYA

RED SEA

PHILIPPI

MACEDONIA

PHARSALUS

ACTIUM

ATHENS

AEGEAN SEA

were intricate and rested upon a subtle, shifting balance of power. Its civilization was graceful, learned, and critical. On the surface it displayed lavish richness, but underneath was the vital problem of the interaction of Oriental and Greek systems of thought and organization. The Hellenistic world held and transmitted to Rome much more of the Orient than one might suspect at first glance.

Hellenistic Politics and Economy

Politically the Hellenistic world included all the shores of the eastern Mediterranean and extended into Asia as far as the Iranian plateau. Within this area the three main states in 264 were Egypt, Syria-Mesopotamia, and Macedonia. Smaller districts were held by such powers as the rising state of Pergamum in Asia Minor, the great trading city of Rhodes, and two leagues of Greek city-states, the Achaean and Aetolian. The major states were ruled by Macedonian stock and were largely governed by fortune-hunting Greeks, who poured out into the East after Alexander. With them they brought their insistence upon a rational approach to all problems, and in many areas broke down the traditionalism of the Orient. Hellenistic Egypt was a marvel of centralized state planning, but in the end it still resembled the Egypt of the Pharaohs more than a city-state like Athens. Hellenistic states were large, and they were in almost all cases autocratic; this age introduced into western civilization the Oriental concept of the divine ruler. Yet at the same time these kings did their utmost to promote Greek culture, at least down to 200; then the effort at Hellenization ran into political difficulties as the natives began to react more strongly.

Economically Greek rationalism improved both agricultural and commercial techniques of the ancient Orient. The peasants on the Nile now gave up their stone hoes for tools of iron. Wide areas began to use money in trade for the first time, and commerce reached the height of its specialization during the ancient world. But, at base, the Orient still lingered. Unlike the small, individualistic trader in Greece, the Hellenistic trader was often an agent for a king or big landowner. Land itself was not held in small sections as in stony Greece but in great estates; and the plantation style of farming tended to spread, first into Greece itself, then into Roman Italy, with tremendous political and social effects.

Hellenistic Culture

In this period the system of classical education, built around grammar, dialectic, and especially rhetoric, was refined and widely spread. Hellenistic authors were more deft at criticizing and evaluating the past than in creating new works of enduring value, though a great deal of popular and learned literature was produced. Overly refined, replete in mythological allusions, striving for originality, most Hellenistic literature lacks depth of real feeling and so betrays its artificial social and cultural base. Similarly Hellenistic art, though based on conventions and techniques of classic Greek art, is far more realistic, is inclined to explore the pathetic, and is overly forceful in emotion. Technically, however, the poets and sculptors of this period were very competent. They had a great influence on Roman culture, for Rome, it must be remembered, met the Hellenistic world, not the classic Greek era, when it expanded eastward.

In essence the Hellenistic may be distinguished from the classic Greek as being more cosmopolitan, more polished, less original. Nevertheless it was not entirely without force and originality in some fields. Hellenistic science is one of the great stars in the crown of the Greek genius. One can do little more than name such men as the geometer Euclid (c. 300), Archimedes the mathematical physicist (c. 287–212), or Aristarchus (c. 310–230), who guessed that the earth went around the sun. Even more distinguished in their day were the versatile scholar Eratosthenes (c. 275–194), who measured the circumference of the earth by a truly scientific method and with remarkable accuracy, and Hipparchus (c. 190–126), the greatest Greek astronomer, who invented trigonometry in his efforts to correct earlier astronomical and geographical research. In mathematics, geography, and astronomy the Hellenistic advances were spectacular, as also in medicine, where dissection was carried out at Alexandria. These scientific developments had little connection with the practical techniques of industry; motivated chiefly by intense curiosity, the scientists of the Hellenistic world used logic as their main tool, but did employ experiment and the collection of information more than their predecessors before Aristotle.

Hellenistic developments in philosophy, again, were notable and had a tremendous influence on Roman thinking. The problem which met the philosophers now was an urgent and serious one: thousands upon thousands of Greeks had left their small city-states, where they were supported and strengthened by local ties and customs, and were now living in the cosmopolitan society of the great Hellenistic states under absolute rulers. These uprooted Greeks needed some form of guidance in life under the new conditions.

Of the numerous answers given, Epicureanism and Stoicism became the most famous. Epicurus (342–271) was a gentle soul living at Athens, who felt that his fellow man was afflicted by superstition and fear. To remove these terrors he preached a doctrine of materialism. The gods did indeed exist, but they paid no attention to mortals; all the world, including man, was formed by the accidental collocation of atoms. When a man died, his body dissolved into its atoms. So why fear what happens now or in the future? The main aim in life to a sincere Epicurean was intellectual pleasure, to be gained by a simple life of retirement from the problems of the world.

Contemporary with Epicurus was the gaunt Zeno (335–263), who walked up and down the Painted Portico (*Stoa Poikile*) at Athens, expounding the Stoic philosophy. Unlike the fixed Epicurean system, Stoic thought changed considerably in later generations and eventually absorbed a tremendous portion of the main concepts in ancient thinking; in Rome this philosophy was to be of far-reaching significance, and it later influenced Christian leaders. To the Stoic the world was governed by the divine spirit. Man had a spark of the divine in him, and it was up to him to lead an active life in this world so that the spark might go back to the divine upon his death. Essentially the only good and evil was within one's mind, for the body was mere dross; anything that happened to it, accordingly, was incidental—the Stoic, indeed, could argue that all events were in accordance with divine will and were for us to accept and understand. His was a life of duty; and since all men equally had a spark of the divine, they were essentially his brothers, or fellow citizens in a great world state.

Despite its originality in science and philosophy, or its technical skill in art and literature, Hellenistic civilization did not have a long bloom. After 200 B.C. decay becomes apparent in one field after another. Astronomy turned into astrology, geography became purely descriptive, medicine stressed the empirical rather than the inquisitive, Oriental religions gave a nonrational answer to the world's problems which began to rival that of the philosophers. The reasons for this change are hotly debated. There can be no doubt that outside pressure weighed heavily, the Romans pressing in from the west, such peoples as the Parthians advancing from the east; for certainly the Roman conquest was brutally destructive of Hellenistic economy. But as one studies the record of war among the Hellenistic states after 250 B.C., one cannot but feel that these states first tore themselves to pieces by their own rivalries. Nor may one forget that few of the states had attained an internal balance between Greeks and natives. Yet, though the Hellenistic world invited— almost required—conquest, the power of the Greek tradition, as encased in its Hellenistic form, has never been better shown than in its terrific effect upon the political conqueror. Looking back from the age of Augustus the poet Horace rightly exclaimed that "Greece, the captive, made her savage victor captive, and brought the arts into rustic Latium."

Rome and Carthage

When Rome began to expand outside Italy, it first turned west. In 265 B.C. the western Mediterranean was divided among three powers—the Roman confederacy in Italy, the various Greek states in eastern Sicily and southern France, and the Carthaginian trade empire of Africa, Spain, and western Sicily. Relations between Carthage and Rome had thus far always been incidental but amicable, and in the 270's the two states were actually allied against a mutual danger, King Pyrrhus. Victory against Pyrrhus, however, had brought Rome down to the shores of the strait separating Sicily from Italy, and through difficulties in Sicily the two greater states soon drifted into war. This First Punic War lasted almost a generation (264–241 B.C.), largely because of Rome's unfamiliarity with the sea. When the Romans did build a fleet and challenged Carthage on its own element, they proved that discipline and daring were as valuable as nautical skill in ancient battle, for they won all but one engagement; but they failed to respect the storms of the Mediterranean and lost fleet after fleet through foolhardiness. During the war something like 500 Roman warships and 1,000 transports went down; at least 100,000 Italians drowned. Bled white, the Romans and their subjects could only grope groggily for a few years after 250, but then in one last dogged spurt they built another fleet, and the war ended. Rome gained control over all Sicily plus an indemnity.

After the First Punic War Rome conquered the Gauls in the Po Valley, gained a protectorate over the piratical islands on the east side of the Adriatic, and filched Sardinia and Corsica from Carthaginian rule. Spurred by its friend Massilia, the Roman Senate also cast anxious eyes at the Carthaginian expansion in Spain, which was directed after 221 by a young man of noble family called Hannibal. Only twenty-five when he assumed control in Spain, Hannibal (247–c. 183) rapidly proved himself to be an astute politician, an able general, and an implacable foe of Rome. Roman efforts to interfere in Spain eventually produced the Second Punic War (218–201 B.C.), the most severe test which Roman character and the Italian confederacy were ever to meet.

In this war Rome held unquestioned mastery of the seas

and planned to invade both Spain and the Carthaginian homeland. The plodding Roman generals, however, had not taken Hannibal into account. The Carthaginian leader broke across the Pyrenees with his devoted army of Spaniards and Africans in the spring of 218, crossed the Rhone before the Romans could stop him, and made his way over the Alps in the early fall just after the first snows. Once in Italy with 20,000 foot and 6,000 horse, he hoped to rouse the Gauls, defeat the Romans completely, and so shatter the Roman confederacy. In his calculations Hannibal made only one mistake: born and bred in an empire which rested more on force than on consent, he failed to perceive the strength of the ties between Rome and its subjects.

Otherwise all went as he had planned. He enticed the overconfident Roman leaders in the Po Valley into a battle on the Trebia River in the morning mists and utterly defeated them, though the generals got away and claimed a victory. For the next year (217) the populace elected one of its favorites, the demagogue Flaminius, as a consul; Hannibal inveigled him into a trap and destroyed both consul and army. Again for 216 the people insisted upon a popular hero, Varro, while the senatorial aristocracy secured the election of Paullus as the other consul. The Senate by now had begun to fear the effect on Italy of this Carthaginian conqueror and broke its usual policy by directing the consuls to give him battle.

The result was the battle of Cannae in Apulia. On an August day Varro and Paullus led out their large forces (about 60,000) on a smooth, open plain by the south bank of the Aufidus River, facing southwest with cavalry on the flanks and infantry packed tightly together in the center for a power play. Hannibal lined up opposite with some

45,000 men, his larger cavalry force likewise on the flanks and his infantry—Africans, Spaniards and Gauls, and Africans again—in the center, bowed out toward the enemy. In the action the Romans pressed back the Carthaginian center until it was straight, then drove it back yet more. Hot, blinded by a dusty wind, crowded together, the Roman foot pushed on—only suddenly to find Hannibal's Africans wheeling in on their flanks and Hannibal's cavalry, victorious over the Roman horse, coming in behind them. Hannibal's cunning tactics had once more entrapped the Romans and led to the almost complete destruction of the encircled army.

After Cannae some of Rome's subjects in south Italy revolted. The rest, however, stuck with Rome, and Hannibal now began to experience the true strengths of the city. The Romans refused to ransom the captives of Cannae, they took down the arms dedicated in their temples and armed slaves, they forbade the word "Peace" in the city, internal cleavages were forgotten, and above all they made desperate efforts even by human sacrifice to regain "the peace of the gods," the loss of which evidently had doomed their army.

Never again in Italy did a Roman general allow Hannibal to draw him into a full-scale battle; rather, one army dogged his footsteps while others reoccupied the lost territories and took Spain. In 212 the Romans had twenty-five legions under arms in addition to a large navy. In 204 the Roman conqueror of Spain, Scipio (Africanus), invaded Africa and forced Carthage to a truce, during which Hannibal at last left Italy. For fifteen years he had supported his army in a hostile country and had maintained within that army of diverse elements a high level of efficiency. In Africa one last battle remained for him—at Zama in 202, where Scipio turned Hannibal's tactics against him and won the day in a hard-fought action. Carthage then yielded to a harsh peace. Spain became Roman, the Carthaginians lost their navy, and they were forbidden to make war except with Rome's consent.

Conquest of the East

After the defeat of Hannibal Rome held the western Mediterranean under its control. One might have expected peace, for the state and people appeared exhausted by the desperate struggle, which to later generations marked the height of the old Roman *virtus*. Instead, Rome turned east within a year and hurled its armies in quick succession at two of the major powers in the Hellenistic world, Syria and Macedonia. The ostensible cause of the new wars was the appeal of skillful ambassadors from Rhodes and Pergamum: hoping to draw Rome in to redress the eastern balance of power, they played on the dangers to Rome of a reported alliance between the ruthless Philip V of Macedonia and Antiochus III of Syria, who was looming up like a second Alexander. Beneath the surface, however, one can detect the grave effects of the Second Punic War. The Senate, which had been given virtual control of the state machinery as a result of the reverses by popular leaders early in that war, appears to have been warped by an almost hysterical fear complex and showed very poor judgment. A preventive war was first declared against Philip (200–196) "to free the Greeks" and so prevent the kings from using Greece as a base of operations against the Italian peninsula. Philip was defeated, the Greeks were freed, and then Rome found Antiochus moving into the vacuum left in the Aegean. The war against Philip thus made inevitable the war against Antiochus (192–189), which expelled him from the Aegean and Asia Minor.

Rome took no territorial gains from these wars. Its leaders gave Greece a presumably definitive reorganization and seem to have hoped for voluntary support by the liberated Greeks; instead, they found that the Greeks wanted complete freedom and were not entirely grateful to their "barbarian" friends who looted widely and then posed as benefactors. All in all, the Roman Senate failed to understand the complexities of the Hellenistic political system; in turn each faction in the Greek states tried to gain Roman support for its own ends and failed to comprehend both the vigor and the simplicity of Roman thought. The result was explosion after explosion in the middle of the second century until finally Roman patience gave way to irritation and then to open arrogance. In 148 Macedonia became a province, and two years later the Greek states were attached to it as a dependency. Asia Minor, mostly in the hands of Pergamum, was left to Rome by the last king of Pergamum in 133 and also became a province.

Problems of Empire

After 150 B.C. Rome's will dominated everywhere in the Mediterranean, in provinces, dependencies, and technically independent states alike; but Rome was not governing the Mediterranean very successfully. Its vacillating attitude and occasional brutality had had terrific effects on the economic and social system of the Hellenistic East. The Spaniards, rebelling at extortion and injustice, fought one long guerrilla war after another. Carthage was provoked into rebellion and then utterly destroyed (149–146). In Sicily and Italy there were serious slave rebellions; on the seas pirates grew steadily bolder as Rome eliminated the last Hellenistic navies. Just before the turn of the century German invaders, the

Cimbri and the Teutons, broke into Gaul, destroyed a Roman army (105) in the greatest disaster since Cannae, and were only with difficulty beaten when they penetrated the Po Valley. Clearly something was wrong with Rome, but to understand the roots of the trouble we must turn to consider the effects of the conquest thus far.

In the first place the Roman methods of government, though subtly changed by the acquisition of power, did not expand in the right directions. The Romans stumbled into empire. They had very little comprehension of the problems of imperial government and refused to copy the elaborate state organizations of the Hellenistic powers. One underlying difficulty was the fact that the senatorial aristocracy, the main framer of policy after the Second Punic War, was reluctant to enlarge its closed ranks to supply extra magistrates. Twenty-five main senatorial families so dominated the government during the second century that only five men whose ancestors had not held office became consuls from 200 to 146. Though the great, closely-knit families marshaled their tenants and other hangers-on against each other in fierce contests to gain offices of state, these feuds rarely involved serious questions of policy. The Roman state drifted and refused to meet its slowly growing problems; its leading elements concentrated on enjoying the fruits of Hellenistic civilization and on amassing money.

In its new possessions Rome did not introduce the Italian type of alliance which called for soldiers in time of war; instead, it continued the usual Hellenistic policy of requiring tribute from the subject cities. The step was almost inevitable, but thenceforth Italy and the provinces were quite distinct and remained so for a long time. To each province created through 146—Sicily, Sardinia and Corsica, Nearer

Spain, Farther Spain, Macedonia, and Africa—Rome sent each year only an elected, unsalaried praetor, with a quaestor as his assistant. The great bulk of local government was left in the hands of the basic political units, cities or tribes; here Rome tended to encourage the growth of cities and oligarchic control.

Over these governors the Senate had little real supervision. Our general impression is that, once the initial severities of the Roman conquest were past, most Roman governors did a fair job, but they were hampered by a lack of continuity, lack of centralized control, and lack of expression from below. When now and then a rapacious praetor, imbued with the increasing individualism and love of money which appears in second-century Rome, played the tyrant over the provincials, little could be done about it. In 149 the Senate set up a standing court to try such persons, but all evidence suggests that its senatorial members were loath to condemn their fellows merely to please provincials. Equally dangerous with the lack of control over the governors was the failure to provide a standing army and navy for the defense of the empire. Rome had always raised its forces to meet a specific need, and this policy of extemporization was continued even though the needs of the state were steadily becoming more continuous.

Economic and Social Changes at Home

Another field of far-reaching change was the economic. The wealth of Rome not only increased tremendously, it also shifted significantly in distribution. Together with the building of roads, maintenance of public buildings, and so on, the collecting of taxes in the provinces was farmed out by state contract, and the group which tended to specialize in this field became known as the equestrian order. These equestrians gained considerable wealth from their activities for the state and from their wide-scale money-lending activities. The equestrian "publicans" were not noted for being merciful or even just; on the contrary they combined at times with the governors to shear the provincials and charged exorbitant interest rates.

While this element rose rapidly in wealth and significance, the senatorial group still retained its primacy. Debarred by law from state contracts or even commerce, the victorious consuls and praetors put the profits of war and governorship chiefly into land. They thus helped speed a revolution in Italian agriculture—the shift from intensive farming by independent peasants to the creation of large farms under central, scientific management, operated largely by slaves. This revolution, one of the crucial points in the development of Rome, can be detected in its beginnings before the Second Punic War, but it was much assisted by the course of that and subsequent wars. Hannibal's ravaging of Italy put many a small farm out of operation; the system of conscription, which took only property owners, kept men away from their homes for year upon year as the military demands of the empire grew. Again, the wars brought hosts of slaves to Rome; to give an extreme example, in one year one general enslaved 150,000 persons in the area now called Albania. As a technical base for the new type of slave agriculture the Roman landowners adopted the scientific principles of Hellenistic land management. Here the Hellenistic world began to have its revenge upon its conqueror.

By the middle of the second century much of south Italy was devoted to large ranches. Campania, Latium, and Etruria were largely given over to plantations of considerable size,

raising olives, grapes, vegetables, wheat, and other products
as the location permitted. From the economic point of view
the change was an advance, but in its political and social
effects it was catastrophic: the element upon which the state
essentially rested was being rooted out. Some of the small
farmers drifted to the exciting, ever-growing city of Rome;
others moved to the provinces; many settled in the Po Valley,
where small farms were still possible. But in Spain or the
Po Valley these Romans could no longer attend the assemblies, and those citizens who barely kept alive in Rome were
not the best voters from whom to expect independent, careful judgment. Trade and industry in Rome, or in Italy generally, did not keep pace with the rise of the state, for imports
from the Hellenistic world gained the upper hand in many
spheres; in the others, skilled slaves from the East tended to
take over both production and sale, operating for the account
of a wealthy equestrian or senator. Though any free Roman
might swell with pride as he watched the triumphs and saw
new temples and mansions rising, he might have trouble
earning his daily bread in second-century Rome.

While the drift of the poor to the city represented a loss
of incalculable value to the armies and institutions of the
state, the ever-increasing ostentation of the rich could only
harm that class from the point of view of the old Roman
morality. The individualistic tenor of Greek philosophy
began to act as a dissolvent on old Roman group attitudes.
Within the family women became ever more emancipated
and marriage ever less sacred in the old sense; toward the
end of the century one Roman censor soberly urged his
fellows to undergo the necessary evil of marriage to keep
up the population. Changes in moral attitudes must always
be assessed gingerly, but there can be no doubt that social

tensions grew in second-century Rome as the contrasts between rich and poor, free and slave, Roman and non-Roman became sharper.

The Surge of Hellenistic Civilization

The political prominence of Rome and its wealth naturally attracted culture. The ensuing changes in Roman civilization from the mid-third century down to about 133 are of tremendous significance in the history of the state. The onrush of Hellenistic influence began in the third century after Rome's conquest of south Italy and Sicily, but it did not reach full flood until the second, and still more the first, century, when Roman generals and soldiers came into direct contact with the main centers of the Hellenistic world and brought back booty, slaves, and dependents to Rome. It was inevitable that the rather naïve and simple Roman should look favorably upon the luxuries and arts of the cosmopolitan, graceful inhabitants of the East: the Romans had almost nothing of their own in these fields, and insofar as any outside civilization had influenced Rome since the days of the kings it had been primarily the Greek. Yet the degree to which the conqueror bent culturally before the conquered and humbly admitted his inferiority was extraordinary.

The Romans first borrowed means of entertainment and physical pleasure. Bakers, cooks, painters, sculptors, and a host of other specialists appeared in Rome either voluntarily or as slaves, bearing the latest tricks of the Hellenistic world in pampering the body, delighting the eye, or lulling the ear. Particularly significant and somewhat more easily seen is the awakening interest in Greek literature at Rome after 250 B.C. In this field the Romans first took plays, to be performed for the populace on state occasions, and the stresses of the war with Hannibal encouraged the frequent presentation of such drama.

The first writer of note, Livius Andronicus (c. 284–c. 204), came from Tarentum; in his plays he put side by side material from Homer, the Attic drama, and the New Comedy. Succeeding dramatists wrote mainly comedy, though by "writing" one means primarily "translating." Nor did these Roman playwrights merely reproduce one Greek work; since they had a wide field of Greek originals from which to choose and a simple audience with an appetite for heavy doses of amusement, the usual practice was to take pieces from two or three Greek plays, stitch them together, and present the result as one play. Plots in Roman comedy, as a result, are sometimes peculiar. Still, it must be admitted that the Roman writers have a gift for telling phrase and absurd situation which is not merely copied from the Greek originals. The Umbrian Plautus (T. Maccius Plautus, c. 251–184) had a superb sense for dialogue and a broad vein of humor; Terence (P. Terentius Afer, c. 195–159), on the other hand, was more refined and more interested in psychological delineation of character. As he tells us in one of his prologues, his plays did not always please the Roman audience; once a ropedancer set up nearby, and all his audience left to see the more interesting sport.

In addition to comedies, tragedies were also translated and performed, but were less popular. Livius Andronicus translated the *Odyssey*, and the resulting Latin poem replaced the Twelve Tables as the standard text for boys learning their mother tongue. Various poets were also commissioned by noble patrons to celebrate the great deeds of the epoch. Naevius (Cn. Naevius, c. 270–201) thus wrote an epic on the First Punic War, and Ennius from Calabria (Q. Ennius,

239–169) composed a great poem in rugged hexameter entitled *Annales,* which chanted of Roman history from the beginning. In the work of men like Ennius or the Roman senator Fabius Pictor, who wrote a history of Rome in Greek about 200, appears the pride of Romans in their past development and character.

All this literature, together with the numerous originals and copies of Greek art and sculpture which poured into Rome, served to please and divert the Romans or to satisfy their pride. But its effects went much further. Inevitably the surge of Hellenistic civilization into Rome had a considerable, ever-increasing effect upon Roman thought and attitudes toward life. Exposed to the full charm of the civilization when they served in the East, surrounding themselves with its products in Rome, reading and seeing its literature, listening to its persuasive philosophers and rhetoricians, the Roman aristocrats had no native tradition of learning or philosophy with which to stop up their ears and eyes. When a character drawn by Ennius declaimed on the stage:

'Tis my creed both now and ever—there are gods beyond
the skies;
But I hold they never trouble what we human beings do,
Else the good would thrive and villains wither—which is
far from true! [1]

he was voicing a stock thought of Epicureanism, but many a Roman must have gotten a shock which set him thinking about the old gods of Rome.

Yet it will not do simply to say that the Romans took over

[1] Translated by J. Wight Duff, *Cambridge Ancient History,* VIII (Cambridge, 1930), 405 (by permission of the Cambridge University Press).

Hellenistic civilization lock, stock, and barrel. On the contrary the influence of this civilization was curiously limited in several respects. In politics, law, and military matters the Romans seem to have felt that the East had little to teach them. From Hellenistic science the Romans accepted chiefly the practically useful discoveries in such fields as agriculture and medicine. The one field of the arts in which Romans were outstanding, that of architecture, owed much to Hellenistic precepts, but the Romans early became independent; though the Romans did not invent the arch, they made ever greater use of it in their mortar-and-brick work and later developed the dome.

For itself the aristocracy claimed a wide freedom of thought, but it was chary of admitting that freedom for its inferiors, whether in literature, religion, or social activity. In the main it preferred down to the last century B.C. to fight its feuds on its own level and did not look with favor upon appeals to the common people which might result in the loss of dignity by individual nobles. Native citizens of the upper classes did not write plays, and most authors and artists were dependent upon aristocratic patrons both for money and for protection. A man like Plautus was careful to put his displays of sin in another land, and the Romans boasted that their stage did not have the unrestrained license of the classic Athenian comedy. Naevius, for instance, attacked Scipio Africanus from the stage and was put in jail until he recanted. Nowhere in the Roman Republic will one find Romans asserting that freedom of speech is a vital part of liberty; Ennius summed up the situation in a famous line, "It is dangerous for a plebeian to mutter aloud."

The Old and the New

To understand the currents of the second century, after Hellenistic influence was rising in Rome, one could not do better than to study and compare two of its major leaders, Cato the Censor (M. Porcius Cato, 234–149) and Scipio Aemilianus (185–129). Cato came from old country stock and made his way up into the senatorial aristocracy through sheer dogged ability coupled with friendship in high quarters. In his youth he fought against Hannibal and could show scars to prove it; then he opposed Scipio Africanus in the factional strife of the era and eventually drove the conqueror of Carthage into semiexile. Cantankerous, violent in speech, Cato prided himself on being an Old Roman. He opposed the Greek sympathizers in politics, and he struggled against Hellenistic influence in daily life. As censor he tried to cut down the scale of luxury in Rome, even going so far as to rip out water mains laid into private houses. For his son he wrote a truly Roman history "in large letters." One paragraph from this or another work runs as follows:

I shall speak in the proper place, of those damned Greeks; I shall say what I saw in Athens, and how it may be good to glance at their literature, but not to go into it deeply. I shall prove how detestable and worthless is their race. Believe me, Marcus my son, this is an oracular saying: "if ever that race comes to pass its literature to us, all is lost." [2]

One would hesitate to call Cato a fraud, but certainly he was more a creature of his age than he admitted—in fact, he was as thoroughgoing an individualist as his opponents. He learned Greek himself, and many of his famous apho-

[2] Translated by M. R. Dobie, in Albert Grenier, *The Roman Spirit* (New York, 1926), p. 149 (by permission of Alfred A. Knopf).

risms were filched from the Greek. Rather than being simple
Cato really was avaricious and boastful, and though of
rustic origin he was in his age one of the leading practitioners of capitalistic farming on the Hellenistic model. The
earliest monument of Latin prose is Cato's work on agriculture. Politically he was successful in leading the Romans to
adopt a harsher attitude toward the eastern states, but intel-
lectually he failed to stem the onrush of Hellenistic thought
and customs. Cato's defeat here was a victory for later civilization, for though Rome henceforth had no chance to de-
velop a purely native culture, it was to pass on to the medieval
and modern world much of the Greek civilization it acquired
during and after the second century.

Scipio Aemilianus, the grandson by adoption of Scipio
Africanus, flourished at the end of Cato's life and reflects the
adjustment to Hellenistic thought which the aristocracy had
made by the late second century. He encouraged Terence,
harbored Polybius, the greatest Greek historian after Thu-
cydides—whose subject was the rise of Rome—and was the
sponsor of Panaetius, the Greek philosopher who adapted
Stoicism to the Roman pattern of life. The circle about
Scipio Aemilianus, both Roman and Greek, was truly cul-
tured and influenced Roman thought greatly. Yet this same
man was the general who led the Roman army at the final
conquest and destruction of Carthage, the general who
ended one of the bitterest wars in Spain. Cultivated and
thoughtful, such a man still retained much of the old Roman
vigor.

By 133 B.C. Hellenistic culture was coming close to being
dominant at Rome but cannot be said to have impregnated
Roman life. By this date Rome had essentially conquered its
empire, but it had not yet mastered the political, economic,

and social effects of conquest, which were just becoming apparent. The next century, to which we shall now turn, was to be a troubled one, revolving about two main points: a solution to the problems of the empire, both in its government and in its effects at Rome, and a synthesis of the Hellenistic and Roman attitudes toward life.

CHAPTER IV

Trial and Error

THE last century (133–30 B.C.) of the Roman Republic is one of the most exciting periods of the ancient world. The problems are great, and their varied solutions are absorbing. Out of the turmoil rise such figures as Sulla the Fortunate, Cicero of the golden tongue, and towering Caesar—

> he doth bestride the narrow world
> Like a Colossus; and we petty men
> Walk under his huge legs, and peep about
> To find ourselves dishonorable graves.

These are men to kindle the world's imagination.

The century saw the Roman state slide from republic to disguised dictatorship. The Senate, which at the outset united in its hands the major powers of that state, could not control the governors or the tax collectors; supervision within the provinces proper was inadequate; the absence of a standing army and navy prevented adequate defense. The nature of the Roman people itself was undergoing great changes, as we have already noted. In the country the sturdy peasant stock, which had formed Rome's armies, gave way in many districts to slaves, who frequently rose in savage outbursts. The masses of the city, recruited largely from freedmen of the eastern provinces, were unfitted to direct the affairs of state through the assemblies; to them Italy was a stepmother, as one aristocrat contemptuously told them. The wealthy nobles were shifting in character even more rapidly and became rampant individualists. The result was the shattering of the old political structure and the emergence of rule by one man, who could create the necessary machinery of state to restore stability and utilize within it all classes of society.

The Gracchi

Achievement of this solution required a full century from the year 133 B.C., which marks the beginning of the revolution. In that year a young man of the bluest blood, Tiberius Sempronius Gracchus (162–133), was elected tribune. Tiberius was deeply concerned over the disappearance of the rural citizenry, and as a sincere reformer he had a simple, quite conservative solution: a bill to divide the large state holdings of land among the poor. Unfortunately this land actually was in the possession of the senatorial group, who had leased or otherwise obtained it decades before, and since the senators were naturally unwilling to yield their plantations Tiberius faced a bitter fight. To pass his bill he had an opposing tribune deposed from office by the people, an unprecedented step; his stand for re-election to carry out his plans was likewise contrary to custom. Enraged by his threat to their position, the conservatives raised a riot in which they murdered Tiberius.

Their violence postponed the threat of reform for only ten years. In 123 the brother of Tiberius, Gaius Gracchus, was old enough to follow in his steps. Gaius had a more ambitious program. To the conservatives his measure of having the state store and sell grain cheaply to the poor appeared to be bribery, though we might call it social welfare; less justifiable were the vindictive measures promoting the interests of the equestrians at the expense of the Senate and the provincials. Supported both by the mob and the equestrians, he revived the distribution of land, set up a plan of farm-to-market roads in Italy, and began overseas colonization. Re-elected tribune for 122, Gaius dominated Rome for two years. Then the Senate put up a demagogue who outbid Gaius for popular support, the masses turned away when Gaius tried to secure citizenship for the Italians, and on a sad day in 121 there was another riot in which the Senate charged the consuls "to see to it that the republic take no harm." This time the conservative posse killed 3,000 in addition to Gaius. From their confiscated wealth a temple was built to Concord.

It is difficult to feel sympathetic toward the measures of the Gracchi. Their view of the problem was narrow, their answers inadequate, and their reliance upon the assembly against the Senate hopeless. Still, their purposes were noble, and their destruction revealed the intellectual bankruptcy of the conservatives, who were later to rue their introduction of the weapon of physical force. Once the Gracchi were gone, the struggle for power in Rome sank to a lower plane and took on a more violent shape. The rest of the century combines the inevitability of a tragedy with the variety of a circus.

The Gracchi were followed by two political factions called the "best" or Optimates, and the "people's" or Populares; but these pretentious terms really disguised shifting groups and cliques bent on personal success. The Optimates represented the conservative senatorial group, who wished to retain and consolidate the dominant authority of the

Senate. The Populares are less easily to be described; generally their leaders could appeal to the masses, but only when they could also gain the support of the equestrians could they hope for victory at the polls. Their rallying cry was that implicit in the Gracchan program, of wresting power from the Senate. To gain the masses they paraded abolition of debts, establishment of colonies, and reduction in the price of grain. In this epoch of private murder and public purges, dissolution of the Roman state appeared the inevitable result, but from the distance of two thousand years we can see that the Romans were really groping their way toward a more adequate political system. Their empire they were not only to hold in this century but even to expand greatly as a result of the internal quarrels.

Sulla the Fortunate

Nearly all the famous men, including Marius, Pompey, Crassus, and Caesar, posed as Populares. This was the party for individualists, who might hope to gain for themselves the power they took from the Senate. Like most conservative groups the Optimates mistrusted ambitious men, and so only one major figure, Sulla (L. Cornelius Sulla, 138–78), can be found on their side. Sulla, however, is the first great figure of the last century B.C.; as a result of his career the Senate acquired greater powers than it had ever held before or was to hold again.

Though a scion of the old aristocracy, Sulla was born poor and therefore remained obscure until he acquired the wealth of his mistress upon her death. While enjoying the luxuries of imperial Rome, Sulla engaged upon the usual aristocratic career of political and military posts but did not rise to fame until 90 B.C. In that year the Italian allies, who had sought Roman citizenship in vain year after year, finally rebelled. The Romans quickly granted the suffrage they had previously refused and so weakened the dangerous rebellion; then Sulla and others drove slowly into the mountain retreats of the remaining rebels and brought the war to an end by 88. Henceforth all Italy south of the Po possessed Roman citizenship and also tended more and more to be uniform in acceptance of Roman civilization.

Immediately, however, the Italian revolt gave the signal for a serious war in the eastern provinces. In himself the invader, King Mithridates of Pontus, was not a serious threat, but his attack gained tremendous support from the Roman provinces facing the Aegean, which had grown resentful under their misgovernment and now passed from the spread of anti-Roman stories and prophecies to revolt. On one day in 88 the cities of Asia Minor rose and in concerted plot killed 80,000 Italian traders. Before the year was out armies of Mithridates were in Greece, where Athens gladly welcomed the semi-Hellenized king. The danger was very real that this resourceful, daring invader might wrest all the East from Rome.

At Rome two main claimants appeared for the important military command against Mithridates. One was Sulla; the other was the great military reformer, Marius (C. Marius, 157–86). A man of little political sense, Marius was yet a good general who greatly improved the organization, equipment, and training of the legions. His further step of opening the ranks of his army to volunteers was of tremendous significance; thenceforth armies of the Republic were professional. The quality of the soldiers naturally improved, but, since they were deeply attached to the general who raised an army and gave its members their discharge bounties, they were not very amenable to senatorial direction. Another serious result of the change was the fact that generals became steadily more independent in their provincial commands and often had to enter home politics to assure their position and secure state approval for the discharge bounties.

Since the Senate trusted Sulla the more of the two, he was elected consul and soon departed for the East. As soon as he was gone, the Populares marched on Rome, purged in blood a number of their opponents, and terrorized the city for the next four years (87–83) while Sulla was occupied in forcing Mithridates to terms. When Sulla returned in 83, a civil war ensued—the first Rome had ever experienced. Marius was now dead, his lieutenants were inept, and the end was a complete victory for Sulla.

Once in Rome, Sulla extorted unlimited powers as dictator for reorganizing the state. He cynically posted list after list of his major opponents as well as of many whose only offense was wealth; anyone killing a proscribed person could claim the due reward, while the dead man's estate went toward paying Sulla's 120,000 veterans their bonus. This blood-letting once accomplished, Sulla proceeded to his self-appointed task of reform. Some of his measures, which expanded the machinery of government, were excellent and endured, but his deliberate effort to concentrate all powers in the hands of the Senate was doomed to failure. The Senate itself was still an assembly of selfish, money-corrupted nobles beyond any possibility of conservative reform; Sulla himself had partially destroyed the aristocracy in the civil war and proscription. Worse, he had made the army a power in politics and had pointed the way for any ambitious man who wished to gain mastery in Rome.

In 79 Sulla felt his work was done and voluntarily retired.

Cynical, witty, brutal, he yet worshiped Fortune and believed himself a "creature of a superior power." To Sulla the whole world was absurd, and life was meant to be enjoyed without worry over principle. When he died in 78, he left an epitaph for his tombstone: "No friend ever surpassed him in kindness and no enemy in mischief." More fittingly it might have been said that he was at least unselfish enough to try to save the Republic and that at a critical point in its history he shored up the power of the state both at home and in the empire.

The Unrest of the Sixties

Before Sulla was dead ten years, the incompetent Senate had lost the position he had given it. The consuls of 70, Pompey and Crassus, wiped out the last vestiges of the Sullan system and assured the triumph of the Populares. The following decade of the 60's was a floundering period in which the main question was the leadership of the victorious party. The most prominent claimant was Pompey (Cn. Pompeius Magnus, 106–48), originally a protégé of Sulla but now linked with the Populares to get the military posts he desired. Jealous of any superior yet desiring universal respect, Pompey was an able general but politically obtuse. From 68 to 62 he was away from Rome, first to sweep out the pirates and then to deal with Mithridates, once more at war in Asia Minor. In the East Pompey was fantastically successful and engaged in a great reorganization of the eastern provinces.

While he was gone, his ostensible friends feverishly but vainly tried to build up a counterweight to the army he would bring back from the East. Crassus (M. Licinius Crassus, c. 112–53), a man of great wealth, strove to become boss of the political machine. Cicero (M. Tullius Cicero, 106–43) was making his reputation by oratory in this period and endeavored to unite the equestrian and senatorial orders in a "concord of the orders." As consul in 63, he was temporarily successful in welding together his concord of the upper classes in opposition to the serious plot by the reckless bankrupt Catiline. But a permanent union between the purblind gentlemen of the fishponds, as Cicero called the Senators in mockery of their newly acquired passion for raising fish, and the selfish, ruthless equestrians could not last, and it soon fell apart. The entire career of Cicero, leading through glory, exile, and death, is an illuminating commentary on the limitations of a reasonable, essentially virtuous man in times of upheaval.

The Rise of Caesar

Yet another political figure in this decade, though by no means recognized for what he was to become, was Gaius Julius Caesar. The Julian clan might boast descent from Aeneas, the legendary Trojan progenitor of Rome, but Caesar's branch had never produced any great figures. Caesar himself was born about 100 and early showed sufficient ability to earn Sulla's suspicion. Finding it safer to withdraw from Rome, Caesar took the usual postgraduate course of instruction in philosophy and rhetoric at Athens and Rhodes. After Sulla's retirement Caesar passed through the normal chain of offices, spending so lavishly on gladiatorial and wildbeast shows for the populace that he was soon heavily in debt to Crassus. He seems to have acted primarily as an agent for Crassus, in which capacity he acquired a keen perception of the moods of the people. In 63 he was elected *pontifex maximus* (chief priest); thereafter he was praetor and then governor of Farther Spain, where he engaged in some military operations.

If Caesar had died at forty, the modern world would know nothing of him. His life now had only fifteen more years, but events were so shaping that his opportunity had just come. In 62 Pompey returned to Italy and dismissed his army. The Senate thereupon refused to allow bounties for his veterans or to confirm his reorganization of the East. Desperate lest his reputation be ruined, Pompey turned to Crassus, master of the assemblies, and together with Caesar the two formed the First Triumvirate, an extralegal group of three would-be bosses of Rome. Caesar ran for consul for 59, was elected with violence, and then carried out the desires of Pompey and Crassus despite the opposition of the other consul Bibulus; in the end Bibulus retired within his mansion and announced each day that he found the omens bad—a statement which should have stopped public business, but did not. As a reward for his work Caesar received the governorship of the Gauls (Narbonese along the Riviera, and Cisalpine in the Po Valley).

After 59 Caesar began to rise above the level of a machine politician. As governor of the two Gauls, 58–50, he expanded Roman control to the Rhine and the North Sea; in other words he conquered modern France and Belgium and so opened up to Mediterranean civilization the land which was to transmit that civilization through the Middle Ages to the modern world. The conquest was impressive to the Romans, who had feared the Gauls since the sack of Rome. It also had considerable effect upon Caesar's military ability. At the beginning of the conquest his chief power was one of gaining his men's affection; at the end he had not only their hearts but also a consummate mastery of the military art. During the conquest the strength of his army had also risen from two to thirteen legions.

While Caesar was in Gaul, Rome was close to chaos. Crassus sought military glory in his turn by fighting the Parthians in the East but lost both his army and his life (53). Gangs ranged the streets of Rome. Pompey, the only member of the triumvirate left in the city, was slow to act, presumably hoping that all would turn and beg his support. Eventually, after the Senate house itself had been burned in the gang warfare, he was elected sole consul for 52 and quickly restored order. By this time he had an interesting constitutional position. Sole consul, he also was governor of Spain and Libya but acted in the latter capacity by sending deputies or legates out to the provinces. As overseer of the Roman grain supply he likewise operated through deputies. His aim seems to have been to become "first citizen" (*princeps*) of Rome, respected by all elements and particularly by the Senate, for whom he would govern its provinces and control its armed forces. The Senate had a different view of matters. Led by the righteous but politically stupid Cato the Younger, the Senate flattered Pompey and gradually won him over, but the intent was to use him against Caesar and then, probably, to get rid of Pompey himself.

Largely through the unyielding hostility of the Senate Caesar was pushed into a position of rebellion against the state at the beginning of 49. In one rapid rush Caesar pushed down the Italian peninsula, swept aside Pompey's half-formed legions, and forced both Pompey and the Senate to flee to Greece via Brundisium. After crushing the forces led by Pompey's deputies in Spain during the summer—a six-week campaign of brilliant maneuver without a major battle—he whirled back to Brundisium, where boats had meanwhile been built, and crossed to the Balkans before the end of 49. Pompey was still raising an army.

The campaign of 48 is one of the world's military master-pieces and ended in the victory of Caesar's inferior forces at Pharsalus, in Thessaly. Pompey fled to Egypt, where he was killed; Caesar, who followed, met Cleopatra, daughter of the last king, and spent with her almost a year at Alexandria. During this period the Pompeians gained new vigor, and Caesar had further battles in Asia Minor, Africa, and Spain before he could call the Roman world his own.

Caesar as Dictator

Between January 49 and March 44, when Caesar was planning to leave the city again to fight the Parthians, he spent only about seventeen months in Rome itself. This period was yet long enough for him to lay the framework of a masterful reconstruction of the state, though it was not long enough for him to show clearly his plans in their last detail. One principle of his system was that of forgiveness. Having won on the battlefield, he was sparing of his foes and assumed that they would accept the award of war as easily as he. His old army he practically disbanded after the last battle in Spain; his own bodyguard he likewise dissolved. Men who had opposed him, like Brutus and Cassius, he put into office in an effort to unite all parts of the senatorial aristocracy behind his program.

For himself Caesar visualized a position of absolute power for life—the Republic was dead. His supremacy over the Senate was open: he now controlled finances and war, he had the right of expressing his opinion first, once he even received the venerable body while sitting in a golden chair.

He essentially picked the magistrates, though the formality of election was continued. So far all are agreed, but the exact legal nature of Caesar's planned position and the way he intended to use his powers have long been debated. From February 44 he was dictator for life, he had the inviolability of a tribune, he was *pontifex maximus*, and he was overseer of morals. But he apparently wanted more, the place of a Hellenistic king. Thus he secured deification early in 44, when a temple was ordered to his Genius and a month was renamed July. He seems to have desired the title of *rex* or king, which his chief henchman Antony twice offered him publicly in February; but public opinion was hostile to this step, and he was not to have the time to soften it.

Everything that Caesar touched he reformed along logical lines, and the variety of acts accomplished in so brief a time is astounding. He formed a series of overseas colonies to draw off the city poor and resolutely cut the number of recipients of free grain in the capital by over one-half. He reformed the local system of government in Italy along lines which became standard for all the western provinces thereafter. The calendar, which was three months out of adjustment with the solar year, he completely revised; today we still use the same calendar, altered in one small detail by Pope Gregory XIII in 1582. To Caesar Rome and its empire were essentially one cosmopolitan state. He made many provincials citizens and even enfranchised the entire province of Cisalpine Gaul.

Caesar's steps did not secure enthusiastic approval. The well to do were suspicious of his radical followers, and the traditionalists were upset even by such things as the reform of the calendar. Above all, his frank acceptance of autocracy and his cosmopolitan attitude angered many citizens. In all these measures, however, Caesar's dominant characteristic appears: of all great men in history he stands out as a *rational* creature, and as he was driven by his mind, so he expected others to be. The revolution which had brought him into power was ended, and all should accept that fact. Much now needed reforming; Caesar was not the man to pay attention to tradition or custom in his new measures.

Caesar's strength was at once his weakness, for others were not so much rational as vengeful, jealous, or alarmed. On March 15, 44, a band of such men drew close about the dictator as he attended a meeting of the Senate, drew their daggers, and murdered him at the base of a statue of Pompey. "Liberty! Freedom! Tyranny is dead," cried Cinna as he, Brutus, Cassius, and the others ran out, waving their bloody daggers.

While the assassins are beneath contempt, their act was of considerable effect—not in restoring the Republic, for they had made no plans for action after removing Caesar, and in any event the Republic was dead; but in determining the character of the system which was to be. Caesar had in mind a cosmopolitan, autocratic state on the order of a Hellenistic kingdom. His murder and the events which followed were to secure for Rome a system which reflected much more clearly its own lines of political development.

The Rise of Octavian

Caesar's burly, jovial, and self-seeking lieutenant Antony (M. Antonius, c. 82–30) immediately seized Caesar's papers and wealth and began dickering with the Senate and the assassins, who were pardoned but soon found it convenient to leave Rome. Within a month Antony was facing the competition of a youth of eighteen, Caesar's grandnephew. Adopted by Caesar's will as his son, this young man was thereafter called Caesar, but to distinguish him from his uncle-father we usually term him Octavian (C. Iulius Caesar Octavianus, 63 B.C.–A.D. 14). Octavian had been studying in the Balkans but returned immediately on news of the Ides of March. Though inexperienced in politics he was cool and intelligent, yet filled with anger at the murder of the elder Caesar.

Disinclined to accept this callow youngster as an equal, Antony was unwilling to surrender his inheritance or to move against the assassins. Octavian therefore turned to his father's veterans, and on the appeal of his youth and his name quickly raised an army. Complicated maneuvers, largely led by Cicero, soon had Octavian and the Senate fighting together against Antony; Cicero rose to the greatest heights of his career as orator and patriot in hurling his Philippics at Antony during the winter of 44. Cicero's plan was to "elevate and then eliminate" Octavian, but rather the reverse occurred in actual fact. Octavian first extorted the post of consul from the Senate and then joined with Antony in conference. The two agreed with a third leader, Lepidus, to take over the Roman state and govern it with absolute power as the Second Triumvirate.

Late in 43 the joint leaders came down to the city. One of the first acts was to set up a proscription list, to get money and remove enemies; and high on that list stood Cicero's name. After his murder his head was placed on the Rostra in the Forum from which he had often swayed the people, and there Antony's wife jeeringly pierced the dead man's tongue with a pin. In 42 Antony and Octavian proceeded to Greece with an army, met Brutus and Cassius at Philippi, and in two hard-fought battles put an end to the party of the assassins.

The Triumvirs then carved up the Roman world. Antony took the East with the mission of raising money, Octavian eventually held Gaul and Spain, Lepidus received Africa. Italy was to be held in common, but Octavian was assigned the task of settling 100,000 veterans of Philippi on farms in the peninsula. Antony must have chuckled upon securing this division. He held the richest areas of the Roman world; his young colleague Octavian had been assigned a nasty task. So far Octavian had had a meteoric rise, from obscure youth to one of the three masters of the Mediterranean in less than three years, but could he thread his way among the problems now to arise?

At the outset he had to dispossess many of the farmers of Italy to settle his veterans. The result was a rebellion, which Octavian mercilessly repressed. Then he faced Sextus Pompey, the son of the great Pompey, who had gathered a navy after the death of Caesar and now held Sicily and Sardinia. Hostile to Caesar's son, Sextus was blockading Italy, encouraging runaway slaves, and generally acting like a pirate. Octavian's first fleet was destroyed in 38 by storm and battle, but in the following year he grimly set his childhood friend Agrippa (M. Vipsanius Agrippa, 63–12) at work building another fleet in an inland harbor especially constructed for the task. In 36 Sextus was finally smashed.

Octavian had hurdled all his obstacles—first the settlement of the veterans, then Sextus, and always the problem of governing Gaul, Spain, and Italy. The youth was rapidly becoming a seasoned leader; most important of all, he was gradually moderating his ruthlessness and so gaining a great deal of support from the solid classes of Italy. After defeating Sextus, he returned all the captured slaves to their masters; the proscribed who had escaped were generally pardoned; in every way Octavian was indicating that he stood for order, the old Roman morality, and piety toward the gods. There can be no doubt that the years 41–36 were the most crucial in Octavian's career and were the period in which he laid down the lines on which he was later to found the Roman Principate.

Antony, meanwhile, was rapidly losing what support he had in the West. Octavian's propaganda machine painted his failure against the Parthians blackly but did not swing into high gear until Antony threw over Octavian's sister, whom he had married, for the glamorous Cleopatra. While Cleopatra was gaining ever more influence over her lover and then husband, Octavian was destroying Cleopatra's reputation not only for his fellow Italians but for all time to come. When the inevitable war broke out, Octavian had very real support from the West, most of which swore an oath to him as their leader against the Oriental menace. Agrippa directed the armed forces in a masterful campaign (31) which reduced Antony and Cleopatra at the end to breaking out of the harbor of Actium and fleeing to Egypt. There they committed suicide. In the year 30 B.C., as Octavian stood in Alexandria, he was undisputed master of the Mediterranean world. He was the same age as Alexander when the latter died at Babylon; but while Alexander had begun as king, Octavian had started as a schoolboy, his only strengths an adopted name, a cold, native intelligence, and an unswerving determination.

After a year spent in pacifying the East, Octavian returned to Rome to celebrate his triumph and to begin organizing the system known as the Principate, which was to last for three hundred years. In 27 B.C. Octavian received the honorific title of Augustus, by which he was thereafter known. Before considering the new government of Augustus, however, let us turn back and look once more at the period we have traversed, for we stand here at a dividing point in Roman history.

The Synthesis of the Late Republic

From the political point of view the last century of the Republic is outwardly chaos. Political murder began in the days of the Gracchi, civil war and proscription in those of Sulla, gang warfare at Rome in the 60's. The solutions advanced to the underlying problems ranged from Sulla's frank acceptance of senatorial domination through Cicero's reasonable but futile concord of the orders to outright supremacy of one man. Given the primitive character of transportation and public opinion, true representative democracy in our sense was not a feasible answer; in so large a state some form of one-man rule was well-nigh inevitable, and the liberty which yielded to that rule had been essentially the liberty of the senatorial aristocracy. The provinces, the lower classes at Rome, even the Italian middle classes were willing to yield political privileges which they had really not enjoyed so long as their master guaranteed to them stability and prosperity.

In the wild days from 49 to 30 B.C. it may have appeared doubtful if the Roman world were to continue as a unit, but underneath the chaos various things were happening to secure that continuation. One was the reluctant but steady expansion of the Roman political and military machinery from the time of Sulla onward. Another was the unification of Rome and Italy. A third was the ever-increasing yearning of the world for peace lest its civilization collapse. Yet a fourth was the vigorous intellectual outburst of the first century, which tended to unite Hellenistic and Roman in one common culture.

The period from the Gracchi through Augustus is the golden age of Roman civilization. Greece contributed from its long experience a great stock of techniques, motifs, and polished concepts; Rome brought primarily a sense of fresh enthusiasm, practical hardheadedness, and optimistic belief that new triumphs could be won. In art and architecture the Romans settled upon patterns which they explored with considerable ability; form and spirit owed much to Greek influence, but a subtly different interest in the individual, in space, and in nature can be detected in late Republican art. In literature there was a great bloom, which falls into two main periods, the Ciceronian and the Augustan. The storm and stress of the political unrest from the Gracchi down to the death of Cicero rather invigorated than dampened the minds of Roman writers, but the greatest outburst came with the certain security and peace of the Augustan regime. Though the Roman debt to the Hellenistic world is always profound, the Roman stamp yet becomes ever more perceptible in this century as one progresses through Lucretius and Catullus to Virgil and Horace.

One of the most interesting poets of the Ciceronian period was Lucretius (T. Lucretius Carus, c. 99–c. 55), who wrote only one poem, *On the Nature of Things*. That poem, however, is one of the most original and forceful in the history of literature. Brooding deeply on the stress of his times, Lucretius desired to free men from superstition and the fear of death. To do this, he preached the Epicurean philosophy

—that the world was made up of atoms accidentally coming together; that man's soul accordingly dissolves upon death. His poem, in six books, is scientific in tone and inevitably arid in spots, yet the whole is filled with the intense fire of a missionary spirit. Lucretius is unique in the ancient world in his delight in the fierce, primeval forces of nature as displayed, for instance, in an ocean storm. Mocking hatred of superstition, love, and other passions pours out in his lines, and yet he can turn aside tenderly to depict a cow lowing for her calf, sacrificed upon an altar. Reading his rugged verse, one can see that though the material is Hellenistic, the form and spirit are Roman.

In the length of his work and his generally straightforward style Lucretius stood apart from the current trend in poetry, which echoed the complexity and mythological conceits of the short, highly polished works favored at Alexandria. The greatest example of this school is Catullus (C. Valerius Catullus, 84–54). Born in north Italy, Catullus came to Rome and immediately flung himself into the hectic life of the capital. In 116 short poems he reflects the giddy round of that life as well as his deep learning in Alexandrian poetical tricks. Yet his poems are not simply exercises; in these true lyrics appears what one rarely finds in the ancient world— a young soul deeply in love. Unfortunately the Lesbia whom Catullus celebrates was one of the most wicked women in a wicked century; and when he broke with her, his scorn was as hot as his erstwhile love. In his savage attacks on Caesar, Catullus reflected the political tendency of the young poets of the day, but before his early death he had been reconciled to the future dictator.

The overshadowing figure of the period before Caesar's murder is the man from whom the literary era takes its name, Cicero. Varied opinions may be passed on his political career, but in his literary aspect all must agree with the judgment of his contemporary, Caesar, that Cicero had advanced the boundaries of the Latin genius.

Trained in rhetoric and philosophy at Rome and in Greece, Cicero was widely at home in the currents of his age, but above all was an orator powerful in swaying the minds of the Senate and the Roman people. As an orator Cicero set the "classic" Latin style in speeches which are clear, rhythmical, and astoundingly varied to fit the needs of scorn, passion, or appeal. Rome had no great orators after Cicero's death, for the introduction of the Augustan system eliminated the occasion for political oratory. Even under Caesar Cicero was forced to turn from his speeches to the writing of a host of essays and dialogues in the fields of religion, ethics, politics, and rhetoric, all composed in his fluent, graceful style but based almost entirely on Greek sources. In these essays Cicero may be said to have begun Latin literary criticism and to have formulated a Latin philosophical vocabulary; and it is largely due to his work that the Middle Ages and early Renaissance knew as much as they did of Greek philosophical thought.

Nevertheless it will not do to set Cicero down simply as a Greek copyist. Though his mind owed much to Periclean Athens and more to the Hellenistic world, he had no patience with many Greek subtleties; in family customs, in views on government, and less obviously in his concepts of man's place in life this polished, civilized man of the first century B.C. had inherited a great deal from the pattern of Roman thought which had been formed before the Roman conquest of the Mediterranean. Plato's *Republic* is more profound but less practical than Cicero's dream of an idealized Roman Republic, sketched in his dialogue *On the Republic*.

The Augustan Age

Outside of Rome itself and its governing circle Cicero saw but little; his death is a symbol of the passing of the Republic. After Cicero came Augustus with a stabilized political system; after Cicero, again, came a new epoch of literature and art, the Augustan Age, which breathes of an entirely different spirit. This age is one of those rare periods of balance; pride in the past stands over against relief at the present peace and hope for the future. Such a flowering of civilization as occurred in Augustus' lifetime may appear surprising, for Augustus was actually a disguised dictator; but he brought peace, an outward retention of old Roman ways, and also the prosperity necessary to support the arts. The artists and writers of this period were largely supported by Augustus and his deputy Maecenas, but the thoughts they expressed seem essentially to be their own. The almost fulsome praise of Augustus in poetry, prose, and stone as the restorer of stability is yet a sincere representation of popular opinion.

The boast of Augustus that he found Rome in brick and left it in marble was intended metaphorically, but it is not far wrong as a summary of the building program of Augustus and his aides. Arches, temples, theaters, porticoes—the list of what he accomplished is almost endless. Roman architecture profited greatly from this activity, as did also the companion art of the sculptor. In such works of this period as the Altar of Augustan Peace or the Prima Porta statue of Augustus one may sense the same turn back to the spirit of classic Greece, the same pride in the past accomplishments of **Rome**, the same religious thanksgiving for peace and order as appears in the prolific literature of the Augustan Age.

Of these authors, Livy, Horace, and Virgil best illuminate the major ideas of the age. Livy (T. Livius 59 B.C.–A.D. 17) dedicated his life to writing the history of Rome down to his time and has some claim to being considered the greatest of the Roman historians. His standards of criticism were not high, but his style was admirable. He was filled with a love for the old Roman character and so produced an epic work which fixed for the future the traditional view of the Republic. Livy may be said to typify the backward-looking aspect of the Augustan Age; his history is an unconscious admission that the Republic was ended. New things were beginning, but to see what they were one must turn from Livy to the poets Horace and Virgil.

Horace (Q. Horatius Flaccus, 65–8) was the son of a freedman but received the best possible education. He fought at Philippi in the army of Brutus and Cassius, then came back to Rome, where he eked out a poor living until Maecenas began to support him at Virgil's suggestion. In variety of meter and deftness of expression Horace is Rome's outstanding poet, and his thought ranges widely over the whole of society. More personal than Virgil, he now satirizes mockingly the foibles of his world, now praises a lovely lady in a stirring ode, and again gives serious advice on literary criticism or the art of poetry. Often he withdrew from town to his Sabine farm. In his cosmopolitanism, satirical spirit, and delight in leisure he struck notes which have always made him the special favorite of aristocratic societies. Still, he could sing in more serious vein, and some of his odes are stirring evocations of the old religious and patriotic attitudes which Augustus was trying to revive.

Virgil

The other great poet of the Augustan Age, Virgil (P. Vergilius Maro, 70–19), was a gentle soul with sensitive spirit, who yet reflects in his writings the main forces of Roman life and thought. To understand the Roman and his civilization one cannot do better than study Virgil. In itself his life is not exciting. Born near Mantua, close to the Alps in north Italy, he received a good education at nearby centers and then at Rome, but might have remained a gentleman farmer all his life had not the unrest after Caesar's death struck him a rude blow. While Octavian was settling the veterans of Philippi, Virgil lost his farm in the general confiscation; by an appeal he may have gotten it back eventually, but thereafter he lived in Rome or near Naples in the circle of Maecenas. The rest of his life was devoted to his poetry. He died before his greatest work, the *Aeneid*, was completed; his request that it be burned was vetoed by Augustus, who stepped in to save this epic celebration of the Augustan Age. In addition to minor early poems Virgil also produced ten brief *Bucolics* and four books of *Georgics*.

The *Bucolics* are artificial praises of the pastoral life, in imitation of Theocritus' *Idylls*. They display Virgil's tremendous learning, whose roots cannot always be traced, and his skill at imitation of Alexandrian originals; yet not all is copy. The poet's native, lush plains with slowly winding rivers can often be detected in the background, and his love of nature and deep sympathy with misfortune are instinctive. In the *Fourth Bucolic* Virgil sings of a child to be born who will end the strife of the era and in his dreams makes manifest the yearning of the whole period. The child apparently was born to a noble Roman house, but Christians later took it to be Christ and so considered Virgil a prophet of the coming of the Messiah.

The *Georgics* are a handbook on agriculture in verse, composed at the request of Maecenas and intended to further Augustus' program of reawakening interest in farming. To the modern world, city-bred or accustomed to mechanized farming, the *Georgics* may often seem to drag in their technical detail despite their marvelously turned hexameters and glowing digressions, but even now they convey something of the unremitting toil of peasant farming and the rich pageant of the Italian agricultural world with its love of the soil and its festivals. The *Georgics* celebrate Italy as a whole:

Hail, great mother of harvest! O land of Saturn, hail!
Mother of Men! For you I take my stand on our ancient
Glories and arts, I dare to unseal the hallowed sources
And sing a rural theme throughout the cities of Rome.[1]

The theme may have been suggested to him, but Virgil's love of his native land, torn by strife after the death of Caesar, shines forth again and again, as in the following bitter lines:

For Right and Wrong are confused here, there's so much war
    in the world,
Evil has so many faces, the plough so little
Honour, the labourers are taken, the fields untended,
And the curving sickle is beaten into the sword that yields not.
The wicked War-god runs amok through all the world.

Virgil's greatest poem is his *Aeneid*, composed after Augustus had restored stability to this war-ravaged world. The hero, Aeneas, appears first in Homer's *Iliad* as a member

[1] Quotations from the *Georgics* are in the translation by C. Day Lewis (copyright 1940, 1947, by Oxford University Press, Inc.).

of the Trojan royal family, a doughty fighter particularly marked for his piety. A myth early arose of Aeneas' voyage to north Greece, then to Sicily, and finally to Latium, where he became an ancestor of the Romans. This extension of the legend, concocted mainly to give the Romans some tie with the Aegean world, was an inconsistent, uninspired tale when Virgil seized upon it as a subject for his great epic poem.

At the outset of his work Virgil states his purpose: he proposes to tell of the tribulations and wanderings of the man who was directed by the gods to pave the way for Rome. Aeneas carries with him the images of his family gods, the Penates, who are to become the inner gods of Rome and the guardians of its rise. He also brings the idea of a city with "justice, and magistrates, and the august senate." But the *Aeneid* is actually more than the story of Aeneas; through this device Virgil is able to state his lofty views of the development of the Roman Republic. In great passages of prophecy Jupiter, Aeneas' father Anchises, and others step forward to sketch boldly the purpose of Rome and the majesty of its power. The height toward which all Roman history ascends inevitably is the poem's own age, the age of Augustus. Thus the *Aeneid* is a blend of the mythical and the historical, of the past and of the immediate present. Like Livy, Virgil looks to the past of Rome with swelling pride; unlike the historian, Virgil also turns and looks forward into the future with equal certainty of Rome's mighty purpose.

The whole epic is much indebted to Homer's work, both in details of poetic style and in general division. Books I–VI of the *Aeneid* describe Aeneas' wanderings from Troy to Carthage, where he is succored by Queen Dido; and thence to the shore of Italy, where his visit to the underworld is recounted in the great blaze of allegory and religious suggestion of Book VI. All this is modeled on the *Odyssey;* the last six books, describing the settlement of the Trojans in Latium and their wars, reflect the *Iliad*. As an epic the *Aeneid* is inevitably much more artificial than Homer's work; for Virgil lived in an advanced age, and again he was a Roman. The hero is not a half-barbarian Achilles capable of paroxysms of undisciplined anger, but "pious Aeneas." Aeneas, it must be confessed, is not a character who appeals to the modern mind. Throughout he is a creature of the divine will, and one who needs considerable stiffening to keep to the mark. But to a Roman this characteristic merely showed his divine guidance, and in the *Aeneid* he is ever more clearly driven by the divine mission of paving the way for Rome. *Pietas* was one of the great foundations of Roman character, and that quality Aeneas had in great abundance.

It will not do to compare the *Iliad* and the *Aeneid* on any but the most restricted of points. The *Aeneid* is a Roman poem written for a definite purpose, and Virgil packed into it a wealth of learning about Roman religious and social customs. Above all, the poem is infused with Virgil's sense of Roman destiny, which made that state the inevitable master of the Mediterranean—not for plunder or rapine, but for peace, order, and the growth of equality among the races. As Anchises prophesies to his son, the Greeks may excel in sculpture, oratory, or science:

be thy charge, o Roman, to rule the nations in Roman empire; this shall be thine art, to ordain the law of peace, to be merciful to the conquered and beat the haughty down.[2]

[2] Quotations from the *Aeneid* are in the translation by J. W. Mackail.

Rome had a sacred duty, which brought it external empire but culminated in the age of Augustus. Jupiter so states early in the poem:

To these [Romans] I ordain neither period nor boundary of empire. I have given them dominion without end. Nay, harsh Juno, who in her fear now troubles earth and sea and sky, shall change to better counsels, and with me shall cherish the lords of the world, the gowned race of Rome. . . . From the fair line of Troy a Caesar shall arise, who shall limit his empire with Ocean, his glory with the firmament, Julius, inheritor of great Iulus' name. Him one day, my care done, thou shalt welcome to heaven loaded with Eastern spoils; to him too shall vows be addressed. Then shall war cease, and the iron ages soften. Hoar Faith and Vesta, Quirinus and Remus brothers again, shall deliver statutes. The dreadful steel-clenched gates of War shall be shut fast; inhuman Fury, his hands bound behind him with an hundred rivets of brass, shall sit within on murderous weapons, shrieking with ghastly blood-stained lips.

Simply as planned epic the *Aeneid* would scarcely have gained its fame. It reflects once more Virgil's intense love of Nature, but even more it is infused with his deep sympathy and brooding upon the world. His compassion for Dido almost carried him outside the due bounds of his plot but led to the creation of one of the most striking female characters in ancient literature. In the *Aeneid*, more than anywhere else, Virgil is a universal poet, appealing to people of any age. Dante chose him as his guide in the *Divine Comedy*, and his work enjoyed almost religious respect throughout the Middle Ages. The *Aeneid* may be an artificial epic, but it is great in the poetic sense; its place is secure as long as the Latin hexameter is understood.

In Virgil, as in Horace, Livy, or the sculptors of the

Augustan Age, one can see that the Romans had found themselves again, after two centuries of political and cultural upheaval. They had changed considerably from their forebears of third-century Rome. The conquest of the Mediterranean led first to a collapse of the old Republic and then to the evolution of a new machinery under an almost absolute ruler, which we shall soon inspect. The old Roman simplicity gave way to a much more complicated civilization in which Greek culture was fully accepted and integrated. "Rome" no longer meant a dominant city-state but all Italy under Augustus; the next step was to make "Rome" equal the entire Mediterranean.

The Augustan Age thus marks the final achievement of a cultural synthesis between Greece and Rome and the establishment of a stable political system which would safeguard the working out of that synthesis in a truly Mediterranean civilization and its expansion throughout the Empire. And, in closing this chapter, it might be well to note that the Greeks on their side had by now grown ready to accept Roman rule. For a Rome conscious of its mission and an empire reconciled to its domination the future looked bright toward a peaceful expansion and intensification of civilization.

CHAPTER V

The Synthesis of the Empire～～～～

THE new era of Roman history which begins with Augustus is usually called the Empire, and the series of individuals who controlled the state after Augustus forms the famous line of Roman emperors. Though the Empire has a long history running down into the fifth century after Christ, we shall be concerned here only with the period from Augustus to A.D. 180—the two centuries which witnessed the ever more complete synthesis of Mediterranean civilization and its spread through much of Europe. This epoch is one of the great consolidating periods of world history, in which the contributions of Orient, Greece, and Rome were summed up and passed on to later civilization.

These two centuries of uninterrupted tranquillity are perhaps the longest period during which the civilized world has known peace and felt a sense of security. They were gained for the Roman Empire by the Augustan reorganization of the ramshackle, haphazard structure of government built up in the Republic, for the Augustan system lasted without major outward change down to A.D. 180. The nature of the civilization fostered by the famous "Roman peace" we shall examine later. but first let us cast a brief glance at the Empire itself.

The Constitution of the Empire

In one light Augustus is one of the most coldly calculating and consciously opportunist politicians of all time; yet rarely have the conscious and unconscious drives of man been so intertwined and difficult to determine. Though the system of government he established was essentially that of one-man rule, it was not an outright autocracy of Oriental or even Hellenistic character. Augustus had learned too much from Caesar's fate to make that mistake, but he was also a true Roman who sensed the strengths of the Roman character as reflected in its political institutions. In his fight against Sextus Pompey and Antony he had won upon a program of restoring peace and order, but he had also stressed the restoration of the old system of government and the reinvigoration of traditional Roman moral and religious customs. In part this program was designed simply to gain support; in part it reflected his own views about the nature of Roman society.

In 27 B.C. he formally restored the Republic, so ending the era of revolution and illegality, and thenceforth he accepted the principle that the fount of all power was the people. Consuls, tribunes, and other magistrates were elected year by year, as in the old days, for centuries to come. In one sense, then, it is not correct to use the terms "empire" and "emperor" to describe the Augustan system and its director, for the republican machinery technically continued. Though hereditary succession was actually common in this system, each ruler received his collection of purely legal powers anew from the Roman people, and his position might be compared to that of Mussolini or Stalin in modern times. It might be better to give Augustus the title he himself used, "first citizen" (*princeps*), and to call his system the

Principate; but accuracy must yield here, as so often, to custom.

To those Romans who were born in the days of Cicero and became adults under Augustus the new system was intended to mask absolute power with a constitutional guise. In appearance it was a delicate balance between two elements, the *princeps* and the Senate. The Senate's very genuine and far-reaching powers arose partly from a desire to appease the aristocracy, partly from the effort of Augustus to divide up the great task of running the Mediterranean world, partly again from his wish to tap the sources of strength in the old Republic. The Senate thus retained outward control of finances, though the treasury was often dependent on the ruler's private means, which were already great and steadily grew thereafter. The Senate governed Italy, which Augustus stressed as the dominant region in the Empire. It split the provinces with the *princeps*, the Senate taking the more peaceful areas. It began to absorb powers of legislation and justice which later led to the practical abolition of the assemblies.

The *princeps* had sufficient legal powers to check and control any other part of the machinery; he also controlled the armed forces; but in addition his position rested on his *auctoritas* or "authority," a supralegal power arising first from general respect for Augustus' achievements and then in later reigns from the feeling that the *princeps* bound together the Roman Empire. Through his own deft policy Augustus successfully enlisted the aid of all elements of Roman society and bound them to his regime. To gain preferment or even to be admitted legally to their particular class the young nobles and equestrians were forced to turn to the *princeps*; though class distinctions were steadily sharpened, Augustus opened the way for many men of the Italian middle classes, like his friend Agrippa, to rise to high posts. A biting critic, such as the historian Tacitus, might well call this situation "slavery" and moan over the disappearance of liberty, but only through support of the ruler could the ambitious rise to honors.

The old republican offices were reserved in the main for the senatorial families; the higher military and provincial posts went to senators and equestrians, who were now paid. Since they were more carefully supervised than in the Republic, government in the provinces thenceforth was on a fairly respectable level. Much of the Empire worshiped Augustus as a present divinity, an earthly savior and protector; this cult of the emperors rapidly became a formal means of binding the subjects together in patriotic reverence and was later to cause the Christians serious trouble.

In addition to improving the supervision of officials outside Rome Augustus also removed another shortcoming of the republican system by enlarging the central administration. The root of this new, ever-growing imperial bureaucracy goes back to the household servants of a great noble; for when Augustus, as such a noble, became virtual ruler, he used his slaves and freedmen to advise him, to watch over affairs, and particularly to supervise financial matters. The imperial bureaucracy thus arose out of much the same background as the civil service of modern European states, which can in turn be traced back to the households of late medieval monarchs. Since the bureaucracy was not bound by republican precedents, it could be altered to suit conditions and grew rapidly into an efficient system for aiding later rulers in many ways.

Augustus was not content merely with reforms of government, for to his troubled Roman eyes the chaos of the past century stemmed largely from religious and moral decay. To bring back true life to the Graeco-Roman religion was beyond the powers of any ruler, but Augustus did at least revive its cults, repair its temples, and keep it going for the next two centuries. His laws discouraging adultery and over-lavishness in meals or promoting childbearing were bitterly opposed, yet were pushed with iron determination. In the end these efforts at moral reform, among the most ambitious ever tried by any western ruler, failed, and Augustus' own daughter had to be banished for adultery.

During the forty-one years of his rule as *princeps* (27 B.C.–A.D. 14) Augustus established the general tone of the Principate as a truly Roman institution, practically conceived to meet practical needs. His house on the Palatine was more ornate than that of an ordinary aristocrat, but his doors were open to all. The ceremony of an Oriental court crept very slowly into Rome, for even 150 years after the death of Augustus we have the description of a *princeps* riding unescorted across the countryside on vacation, helping in the grape harvest, and acting generally as a private citizen rather than as a monarch. Nevertheless the powers of this "first citizen" were very great, resting as they did on armed force, legal position, and even deification outside Italy; and the limits of his actions depended more upon the balance between whim and sense of duty than upon genuine curbs from without.

Throughout the years the powers of the emperor tended constantly to increase in scope and intensity. This absorption of power was only rarely planned by the ruler; more generally it was forced upon him. The *princeps* was efficient and had a good staff—that was the situation in a nutshell; accordingly people turned to him to get things done. The result was the steady though accidental loss of power by the Senate, by the local units of government (the cities), and by individuals, who became more and more subject to state interference. Yet, though the state loomed ever larger, down to A.D. 180 something of the feeling that the individual had a value—one of the great achievements of Mediterranean civilization—was preserved.

The Development of the Empire

When Augustus died peacefully in Campania, his disappointed, aging stepson Tiberius (*reg.* A.D. 14–37) succeeded him without difficulty and was granted for life the powers Augustus had held. Therewith was inaugurated the series of Roman emperors which, embracing as it does mad Caligula (37–41), pedantic yet industrious Claudius (41–54), dilettantish Nero (54–68), gloomy Domitian (81–96), and philosophic Marcus Aurelius (161–180), has ever since captured the imagination of men. The kaleidoscopic picture of the emperors and their scarcely less absorbing wives and mistresses must be passed over here, and in any event the emperors are less important as individuals than as successive units in a steadily developing system of government.

Down to the suicide of Nero in 68 the rulers belonged to the Augustan family complex; then came a year of anarchy in which the frontier armies fought with each other to elevate their commanders to imperial power. The winner, Vespasian (69–79), followed in Augustus' footsteps by restoring order and putting the armies back under control. After the murder of his second son Domitian in 96 came the series of "Good Emperors" of the second century; down to Marcus Aurelius each was childless and so chose by adoption the most eligible senator to succeed him. All paid due respect to the Senate, unlike such bloodthirsty, suspicious rulers as Nero and Domitian in the first century, though actually the Senate became ever more a sounding board for imperial wishes. These emperors of the second century derived from provincial stock and admitted large elements of the provincial aristocracy into the Senate, there to sit beside the best blood of Italy and so represent the Empire as a whole. While the first century was one of friction between emperor and Senate, the second century was a tranquil age.

By the reign of Hadrian (117–138), which perhaps marks the height of the Roman Empire, the imperial system of government had become a complicated, extensive structure befitting the size of the Empire. In theory the ordinary tasks of government were still divided between the emperor and the Senate, but the functions of the latter became steadily more formal. The Senate now elected the consuls and other officials, it passed legislation, it was still responsible for Rome, Italy, and certain provinces. In Rome, however, the heads of the city police and fire brigades, the administrator of the food supply, and even the city governor were appointed by the *princeps*. Italy retained a favored position in that it was free from taxes and conscription; it also furnished half the Senate; but it was for ordinary purposes of administration treated more and more like any other area of the Empire. Under Hadrian the great secretaryships of the central administration, formerly held by freedmen, were handed over to equestrians, who tended to become ever more specialized public servants, some in the armed forces, others in the civil administration. By this time tax farming was largely abolished, and a number of separate financial services collected the inheritance tax on Roman citizens, the manumission tax on freed slaves, the regular taxes, the rents from imperial property, and so on. The funds flowed to the imperial or old senatorial treasuries, but both were directly under the *princeps'* control.

Roman Law

The increasing power of the *princeps* is reflected also in the development of Roman law. Roman law is one of the greatest Roman contributions to western civilization, but to go beyond the flat statement into an analysis of what that law was and why it was so significant leads at once into a tangle of complexities. Briefly, the law built up by the Romans after the Twelve Tables (about 443–442 B.C.) may be said to meet Dean Pound's requirement that "law must be stable and yet it cannot stand still." Roman law was conservative and so furnished a stable base for business operations, yet it did undergo tremendous changes as Rome grew. The annexation of the empire, beginning before 200 B.C., rendered the old system based directly on the Twelve Tables inadequate, but under the leadership of the praetors the Roman lawyers gradually hammered out an improved system which would meet the greater complications of their more civilized life and wider rule. In this gradual process the practical, instinctive bent of the Romans played the largest part, but the lawyers were also influenced in part by Greek rhetoric, which was prominent in their education, and to a lesser degree by Greek philosophy, which occasionally suggested underlying principles. But in the main Roman law was an empirical law, grounded upon actual cases and events; in this respect its development paralleled that of English common law.

Each year the praetor issued his "edict," based upon the

edict of the previous year; in this document he announced what remedies he would entertain for causes at law. In the reign of Hadrian the famous praetor Salvius Julianus codified this praetor's edict, so that it was no longer subject to change. Legislation by the assemblies, which had always been minor, had likewise ceased; but one safety valve for change remained in the form of the *princeps'* power of issuing decrees with the essential force of law. One cannot yet quite say that the will of the ruler was law, but that day was coming. Already the rulers were having a powerful effect on the law, bending it in ever more humanitarian ways so as to protect the weak, the orphans, and the slaves.

The Armed Forces

Throughout the first two centuries of the Empire the internal development of the government and the general prosperity of the people were protected by the armed forces of the *princeps*. Augustus had made the army and navy permanent and had organized them so successfully that subsequent rulers made few changes in his basic principles. The army consisted of legions of solid infantry, composed of Roman citizens; and the auxiliaries, light foot and horse recruited from non-Romans who were given Roman citizenship upon discharge. Service was long-term, running up to twenty-six years for the auxiliaries, so that an army career was a lifetime profession; local militia and arms bearing were as a rule not encouraged by the rulers. Apart from the relatively small praetorian guard to protect the ruler in Rome the army itself was placed on the frontier. This policy assured immediate protection of the boundary provinces, but if once an enemy broke through the frontiers he had a clear field until troops could hastily be brought up from another less threatened frontier. Fortunately the Empire enjoyed interior lines of communication and was not seriously threatened on several points at once during the first two centuries. In any event it probably could not have afforded a standing army much in excess of the roughly 300,000 to 500,000 men required to guard the frontiers.

Roman fleets helped police the frontiers in Europe, which rested on the Rhine and Danube. Other, larger fleets served in the Mediterranean, based primarily on Italian ports. During the first two centuries of the Empire the Roman fleets did not fight a single major battle, so complete was their control; piracy almost ceased to exist, for the only time in history down to the nineteenth century. The Romans never esteemed the navy as highly as the army, but Augustus and his successors must be given credit for realizing that the Empire was based upon the Mediterranean. Only through control of its waters could an area larger in point of relative time than all the world today be held together under one system of government.

The Roman armed forces were remarkably successful down through A.D. 180 in protecting the frontier. Augustus himself used the army to conquer most of the Balkans and to rectify the frontier elsewhere, but he gave up an intended conquest of Germany after a great disaster east of the Rhine. In his advice to his successors he urged that the frontiers be kept as they were on his death. The conquest of all Germany, which might have had tremendous effects in later history, was never again tried, but later rulers added most of Britain, southwest Germany, and the modern Roumania (Dacia). After the conquest of this last region under Trajan (98–117), who delighted in war, his successor Hadrian gave over the offensive and began to stress retention of what the Empire already held. A stone wall was built entirely across Britain to keep out the Picts, and by the middle of the second century the Roman world was encased in an armor of stone or wooden walls or frontier roads which were garrisoned at intervals and patrolled.

Pax Romana

As one looks back over the reorganization carried out by Augustus and strengthened by the following rulers, its general success and evident soundness of basic principles are amazing. The army, the navy, provincial government, the central bureaucracy, the Senate, and the *princeps*—all combined to produce a lasting peace for the Empire. The "limitless majesty of the Roman peace" is indeed a remarkable accomplishment in history. It cannot be said that this peace was deeply appreciated by the Roman aristocracy after the time of Augustus, for they now had lost their opportunities for loot and personal power. The upper and middle classes of the provinces, however, were very enthusiastic and revealed their enthusiasm through hosts of statues and inscriptions set up in honor of the rulers who guaranteed the peace. One of the great triumphs of nineteenth-century historiography was the collection of these inscriptions and the extraction from them of the tremendous amount of information they contain about general conditions in the Roman Empire.

The inscriptions, however, will not entirely answer a vital question which we must now consider: granted that the Empire accepted the *princeps* and so had its peace, what was the real content of that peace? Was it employed to advance civilization to unheard-of heights? And in getting their peace did the men of that period give up anything worth the keeping?

Seneca

The greatest figure in the pagan intellectual history of the Empire is Seneca the Younger (L. Annaeus Seneca, c. 5 B.C.–A.D. 65), whose life and thought both throw a bright light upon the main trends of the period. Few philosophers have had such a chance to direct the politics of their day, for Seneca was both a Stoic philosopher and a member of the highest circles of the imperial aristocracy. Under Claudius he was exiled, and unfortunately for his reputation we have his frantic, bootlicking appeal to one of Claudius' freedmen for restoration to favor; eventually he was recalled by Nero's mother Agrippina, the last wife of Claudius, as tutor for her son. When Claudius died after eating the famous dish of poisoned mushrooms prepared by his wife, Seneca passed from tutor of Nero to chief minister of the whole Empire together with Burrus, commander of Nero's praetorian bodyguard. The period down to 62 in which Seneca and Burrus really ran the state was afterwards remembered as the best part of Nero's reign. Eventually Seneca lost his power and retired. The tremendous wealth which he had accumulated, together with his past position, made him an object of suspicion to Nero, and Seneca's last years were uneasy. In A.D. 65 he and his nephew, the brilliant young poet Lucan, were both forced to commit suicide.

Seneca was more than a senator, a figure of state, or a millionaire. He was also a philosopher of unquestionable sincerity and ability of mind; yet more, he was a masterful essayist with a rushing, choppy, tricky style, a dramatist of repute, an expert in natural science of the period—in short, the most rounded figure of the Empire. If anyone could throw light on the meaning and problems of the Empire, Seneca, both the thinker and the doer, should be that person. At times in his *Moral Essays* as well as in his *Letters* he struck notes of real moral grandeur; at other points he engaged in the most stale rehash of Stoic doctrine; but always he considered directly the ethical problems of the noble class to which he primarily addressed himself.

The inner uncertainty which he reveals for that class, and the resulting worship of Fortune, were in part the result of man's inherent insecurity, but even more it arose from the nature of the Empire. Seneca knew the Principate at first hand. He accepted it and could deliver a strong Stoic argument that kingship was the best form of government (if the king were good):

[The emperor] is the bond by which the commonwealth is united, the breath of life which these many thousands draw, who in their own strength would be only a burden to themselves and the prey of others if the great mind of the empire should be withdrawn. . . . Such a calamity would be the destruction of the Roman peace, such a calamity will force the fortune of a mighty people to its downfall. Just so long will this people be free from that danger as it shall know how to submit to the rein; but if ever it shall tear away the rein, or shall not suffer it to be replaced if shaken loose by some mishap, then this unity and this fabric of mightiest empire will fly into many parts.

Yet the man who had so deep an appreciation of the need for a *princeps* was frequently fearful of the unchecked liberty of action which the ruler enjoyed. To Seneca the Empire was, in the end, a reign of force; all he could do was to hope to bend his young charge, Nero, toward virtue.

With this aim in view he prepared a powerful essay *On Clemency*, whose exhortations to virtue, mildness, and justice he pretended were but a mirror of Nero's own self; but any reader can detect Seneca's real fear as to Nero's characteristics.

Seneca's line of thought is typical of philosophical thinking in the Empire: it is conventional, eclectic, and flat; yet it continues to possess the Roman practicality. In the *Letters to Lucilius*, composed after his retirement, he had become urgent and imbued with prophetic feeling that a man must withdraw from public activity if he were to secure his own true ends in life; liberty was an internal, not an external, political matter under the Caesars. Such was the end of a life of outward glory and wealth! Seneca is often accused of hypocrisy in being fabulously wealthy and yet preaching against the evils of wealth; but Seneca, if any man, could appreciate directly the dangers and troubles of money. The philosophic disdain for this world's goods is coupled with an admission that one of the great aims of life for his contemporaries was wealth:

the whole nation, though at odds on every other subject, agrees upon this [money]; this is what they regard, this is what they ask for their children, this is what they dedicate to the gods when they wish to show their gratitude—as if it were the greatest of all man's possessions!

In this accusation of materialism he strikes a common note of imperial thinking, to which we shall return.

An outstanding aspect of Seneca's thought is his humanitarianism. Among the principal amusements in imperial Rome were the "games," in which animals were pitted against each other, animals against men, or men against men with a good deal of bloodshed and violent death. The public liked the games, which were lavishly provided by the rulers; one satirist coined the phrase "bread and games" to epitomize the policy by which the emperors kept the city populace content and apathetic. Seneca, however, was bitingly opposed to the games where even in the intermissions "men were strangled lest people be bored." Again, he was deeply sympathetic with slaves, for Seneca was as devout as any Christian in believing that each man had a spark of the divine within him:

God is near you, he is with you, he is within you. This is what I mean, Lucilius, a holy spirit indwells within us, one who marks our good and bad deeds, and is our guardian. . . . No man can be good without the help of God.

As Christians of later ages read their Seneca, they were struck by the extent to which he apparently echoed Christian ideas, and it was an easy step in the Middle Ages for people to assume that he had known his contemporary St. Paul and had imbibed his ideas from the missionary of the church; a fictitious collection of letters between the two was even composed and widely circulated. Actually Seneca's humanitarianism and cosmopolitanism rose directly out of the general currents within the Empire, and if Christianity had the same ideas, the parallelism is merely a reflection of the widespread nature of those ideas. Historically considered, the rise of Christianity is much indebted to the preparation of the ground by pagan thinkers. Christianity, indeed, could offer much more, as the case of Seneca clearly shows. Seneca was a humanitarian, but he was also filled with an underlying pessimism and essential apathy characteristic of pagan philosophers. Bred in the rationalistic school of Graeco-Roman civilization which tried to strip away the emotions and rely only on the mind, Seneca could not allow himself the emotional appeal of the Christians. To the pagans, life after death either did not exist—a conclusion which many accepted gladly as marking an end to their troubles—or at best it was a very vague affair as in Seneca. The pagans could not picture a nonmaterialistic afterlife. In yet another particular Seneca reflects the weakness of secular thinking in comparison with that of the Christians. Men were indeed to him all members of one great state, the state of Nature under God, but the individualism of the Roman aristocracy affected him to the extent that a true feeling of brotherly love is not very apparent. Seneca wrote a long work *On Benefits*, but it is essentially an analysis of social duties and good turns on a rather cold plane of the material.

The Culture of the Empire

Further comparison between the Christians and Seneca would lead us away from the Empire itself, but in summation it may be said that nowhere better than in Seneca can we form an estimate of the intellectual level of the Empire. In accepting the imperial system the inhabitants of the Mediterranean did not accept a system which led to great intellectual advances. The nature of the Principate had some repressive weight at times—some authors, too bold in criticism of individual emperors, paid with their lives for their poetry or prose—but the generally stable, unvaried tenor of life in the Empire together with the lack of political voice of the individual probably had more effect in damping down thought than did sporadic political oppression. There is, in other words, a price which men must pay for stability.

The stirring days of the Republic were over; the synthesis

between Greek and Roman culture had essentially been established by the time of Virgil. The Empire thus was notable mainly for the elaboration of that synthesis and its spread into the uncivilized stretches of Europe conquered by Caesar and Augustus.

Beneath the surface the forces which had led to the rise of Mediterranean civilization were ebbing away. Literary men did not have fresh thoughts; instead they turned, like Seneca, to the past and imitated the earlier writers alike in material, in style, and in vocabulary. This decay of ancient civilization was not necessarily as "bad" as it is usually pictured to be; on the contrary, the ancient had to give way if the medieval and then the modern views of life were to be born. Seneca reveals clearly two very interesting points: that ancient thought could proceed no further within its complex of political, social, and economic institutions, and that new ideas were arising which could not be expressed within that complex. Ancient civilization as such might be losing its creative powers, but mankind as a race had not thereby necessarily lost its freshness of thought and originality of concept.

To complete the picture of intellectual activity in the Empire it must be pointed out that, although learning did not progress upward, it certainly expanded outward and downward. Romanization of the Empire we shall consider in a moment, but even in the ancient seats of learning education became ever more widespread. The house walls of Pompeii near Naples, buried by an eruption of Vesuvius in A.D. 79, are covered with scribbled remarks of idlers, obscene and otherwise, by election appeals, by scratched lines from Virgil put down by schoolboys. A very great part of the people of this town could read, and the same was true elsewhere in the Empire. Libraries appeared all over the provinces as well as in Rome. Some cities were hiring public teachers by the second century after Christ, and the emperors endowed regular chairs at Athens and Rome.

One reflection of this interest in education is a work *On Oratorical Training* by the Spanish rhetorician Quintilian (M. Fabius Quintilianus, c. 35–c. 100). A thorough introduction to the art of speaking, which was vital in ancient civilization, it is also an urbane, balanced appreciation of education generally; the author of this work, which was popular down into the Middle Ages, must rank as one of the most independent thinkers and solid judges of the entire Empire. Though learning in the Empire may have been essentially an elaboration of the Graeco-Roman synthesis, such persons as Quintilian, Seneca, the historian Tacitus, the biographer Plutarch, or the witty critic Lucian are still worth the reading, and the era out of which they grew was the most literate until comparatively recent times in modern Europe.

Economic Progress

Both this diffusion of learning and also the manifestation of that humanitarian spirit which marks the Empire rested to a considerable extent upon the great material prosperity of the period. To revert to the question put earlier, one must say that when the Empire accepted the *princeps* and his peace, its principal return was that of physical well-being based on a prosperous economic system. If materialism is enough, then the subjects of the *princeps* had every reason to be happy—down to A.D. 180.

The restoration of peace under Augustus, dubbed "master of land and sea" in grateful inscriptions, gave a great impetus to Mediterranean commerce and industry, the practitioners of which acclaimed in the *princeps* the agency through which "they lived, sailed the seas, and enjoyed liberty and prosperity." In addition to providing peace the emperors built roads, canals, and harbor works, and furnished a good coinage which could inspire business confidence. They also provided a most powerful incentive to trade by their constant expansion of the frontiers in the first century after Christ, for the result was an ever-expanding economy. Imperial encouragement of trade, however, did not in this period extend to imperial control, for the rulers left the business world remarkably free.

The Mediterranean world thus enjoyed those privileges of a tightly knit economic unit which the unrest of the late Republic had interrupted. In general the eastern Mediterranean retained its superiority in industrial skills and provided the more complicated and artistic products, while the western Mediterranean produced raw materials and manufactured items on a lower level of technique. Yet this generalization has its exceptions. Egypt, for instance, provided not only glassware, tricky to make and cherished when obtained, but also great quantities of wheat for Rome. Italy, on the other hand, was a main source of wine for the western Mediterranean, but also captured the market for pottery. To form an accurate picture of commerce and industry one would have to consider the Empire province by province, decade by decade; and the quantity of physical objects left to us by the cities and villas of the period makes such a study almost possible.

Certain main lines of development stand out as the result of the careful research which has been made in this material. It is apparent that the Empire was a hive of industry, whose products spread across the frontiers far into Europe and Asia. Roman coins are found as far as Sweden, and the nearby Germans were considerably influenced by Roman civilization; although they thereby became a greater danger to the Empire, they also grew more likely to appreciate its culture when eventually they did penetrate its boundaries. Another most interesting development, which has its parallels in modern economy, is the diffusion of industrial techniques so that each province could produce its own wares. Not only did crafts proceed from the more to the less civilized areas; they also tended eventually to move from the cities to the villas of large landowners. Thus in Gaul especially we can see that the large country estates were industrial as well as agricultural complexes and that they sold their wares in nearby cities, to the detriment of the economic fabric of the city. Local production was less expensive, but it did reduce the economic bonds holding the Mediterranean world together; the end was to be the reversion to the local economy of the Middle Ages.

The place of the slave was significant in the early days of the Empire, but it tended steadily to decline as the number of captives in war diminished and piracy was stamped out. In the first century the freedman class was large and significant, and our most brilliant (and bawdy) sketch of life in this period, the *Satyricon* of Petronius, is at its best in satirizing the rich, gross freedman Trimalchio, who had made his money and was becoming a landed gentleman. In real life the grandson of such a freedman might become a senator, for wealth spoke loudly in the Empire. The presence of slaves and freedmen is less obvious in the second century; on the farms especially the landlords had long since shifted to free men, termed *coloni*, who rented sections as sharecroppers or on fixed payments. These *coloni* tended to fall under the thumb of their landlord in all respects, but the humanitarian rulers of the second century occasionally intervened to redress the balance—the medieval manor is in the background but was not to appear for some time yet.

Romanization

The general result of the material prosperity of the Empire was the rapid spread of Romanization throughout its lands and seas. Romanization is best defined as the unconscious acceptance of Rome as parent state, for it proceeded on different lines in East and West. In the eastern Mediterranean men already enjoyed a high level of civilization—the Hellenistic—and did not yield to Roman ways. Nevertheless such easterners as Plutarch (c. 46–after 120), writing parallel lives of Greeks and Romans without any prejudice on either side, may be called Romanized even though he did not use the Latin tongue and urged his fellow Greeks to retain their own culture. In the eastern seas only the Jews, buttressed by their faith that they were the Chosen People and by their doctrine which placed religion above the state, consistently refused absorption into the Roman political structure. Trouble between Romans and Greeks on the one side and Jews on the other led several times to bloody revolts of the Jews, which eventually in A.D. 135 brought the complete destruction of the Jewish political state in Palestine.

In the western Mediterranean, on the other hand, the inhabitants were generally on a lower level of civilization than the Romans. Here Romanization accordingly implied acceptance not only of Rome as fatherland but also of Roman civilization proper. This process is of tremendous significance in the later history of Europe; Mediterranean civilization was spreading to northern Europe, and in a Roman guise.

Only to a limited extent was the Romanization of western Europe the result of official pressure, even though the government naturally favored the development. In the main the provincials accepted Roman culture of their own free will because they felt it to be superior, because their own culture was weak, and also because they grew to accept Rome as the natural focus of their system. Important as agencies of transmission were the army and commerce. Approximately one-half the army, the auxiliaries, was recruited from non-Roman provincials. In their twenty-six-year term these soldiers learned to speak Latin, to worship Roman gods, and in most ways to appear Roman. The army was stationed in camps along the frontier, which served as powerful attractions for traders; around the camps grew up trading settlements, and eventually cities often arose on the sites of old camps, as at Cologne, Augsburg, and so on. The camps also required large quantities of nearby grain and so encouraged local chieftains to shift to production for market. To transport supplies and also to assist speed of military movements the army built roads and canals throughout the frontier districts which opened the way to commercial expansion.

One result of the Romanization in the West was the destruction or weakening of local cultures and the ever-increasing uniformity of life as reflected in the pottery and other objects which have survived. The provincials of Gaul, of Britain, and of the Danube lands were doing as much as they could if they pulled themselves up onto the level of civilization already attained by Italians, and one finds little advance beyond that point emanating from the newly civilized areas. Now and then in an inscription an earlier form of religion shows through, either in Roman guise or in its barbaric form; sometimes provincial sculpture betrays a non-Mediterranean way of looking at life; but on the whole the more progressive provincials tried to be as Roman as they could. The result was remarkably uniform and, it must be admitted, rather dull.

In men's minds the reflection of Romanization can be seen in the meaning of the term "Rome." Originally the word described a small city-state on the Tiber; by the time of Augustus it included Italy; but by the second century after Christ "Rome" means the Mediterranean world as a whole. "Roman" emperors are born in Spain or Gaul as well as in Italy; "Roman" authors and officials may hail from Britain, Greece, or Syria.

The Cities of the Empire

Externally the great mark of Romanization was the rise of cities all over the Empire. In Italy the remarkable remains of Pompeii, Herculaneum, and Ostia are well known, but even more impressive to the imagination are those cities of Tunisia and Libya which rose in previously almost desert areas, flourished through the Roman rule, and fell into permanent ruin as soon as the Roman state was ended. In barbarian Britain, at the farthest end of civilization, there were cities; along the Rhine and Danube a crown of cities arose from frontier camps and served as leaders to a thriving countryside; even in Asia Minor the Roman Empire completed the city-founding work of Hellenistic rulers. Only in Egypt, the milch cow of imperial finances, were cities discouraged.

This development of urban life in the Empire is significant

when one remembers that Graeco-Roman civilization was the civilization of the city (*civitas, polis*). Again, the government of the Empire rested squarely on the cities—one may even say the Empire was essentially a union of cities, held together by the imperial framework. The emperor and the provincial administrations, that is, furnished military protection and settled intercity problems, but the great bulk of government was carried out by the city proper. An ancient city held control over the surrounding countryside so that it would territorially correspond more to an American county than to a simple urban district. Along the fringes of the hills or other uncivilized areas, wide districts would be "attributed" to a city, i.e., handed over to the city for local supervision of their government.

The system of city government varied in details, but everywhere the main organs were three: annual magistrates, an advisory body chosen for life, and an assembly of all citizens. The city was governed by its own locally chosen officials, and in the first century after Christ the competition of the wealthier townspeople for the honor of serving as mayor (*duumvir, archon*) was intense. On the walls of Pompeii we can still see the election appeals, but even more successful than appeals were promises to improve the streets, to build a gymnasium, to give games at the candidate's expense. Certainly the liberality of the rich toward their native cities, whether occasioned by ambition or by generosity, was on an order which can be matched only within the past century of western civilization.

In the West these relatively new cities conformed to a general pattern. In the center was the Forum, an open space crowded with statues to city benefactors, governors, and emperors. About it would be a colonnade for walks in the heat of the sun, interrupted at one end by the local temple to the Capitoline triad of Rome, the protectors of the Empire. Other buildings fronting on the Forum might include the local council house, guild halls, markets, and a center for the official worship of the emperors. Elsewhere through the city would be public baths in profusion, temples to old gods of Greece and Rome and new gods of the Orient such as Isis or Mithras, gymnasia, a theater or two, and a huge amphitheater into which most of the town and neighboring population could pour to watch men and animals die in the games. And enfolding all these greater edifices, binding them together, were the paved streets on checkerboard pattern, the tiny shops, and the mass of houses and apartments in which the citizens enjoyed their wealth. There was grinding poverty too, but it slunk away to the corners or escaped into the open fields where the peasants wrestled with the soil. From the material point of view these cities of the Roman Empire represent the apogee of ancient civilization.

Problems of the Empire

It is peculiar perhaps, but nevertheless understandable, that at the height of the Empire one can yet detect serious flaws in its structure which led eventually to its decline. The working out of the factors which accompanied the famous decline and fall of the Roman Empire will fall to the next essay, but our picture of the second century will be incomplete if we do not look briefly at the situation at this time.

The cities began to run into difficulties in the second century. The enthusiasm for electioneering dropped off as economic conditions subtly began to worsen, and we hear of candidates being chosen and elected against their will, then required to carry out the usual good deeds and bear the administrative burdens of an undesired post. The inner contradiction between the democracy of the cities and the autocracy of the central government was gradually removed, first by the shift within the cities toward oligarchy and then by the far more serious tendency of the imperial government to sap the autonomy of the cities. Because of overexpansion and other reasons cities sometimes could not balance their revenues and so received temporarily a financial expert from the emperor, either at their own request or because the ruler was concerned over the revenues which the cities collected for him. As the century wore on, what was temporary at the outset frequently became permanent, and though by A.D. 180 the cities in the main were still running their own affairs, they were steadily more subject to directives from the imperial administration and to inquisition by the provincial governor.

The resilience of the cities and their citizens, in short, was waning. When one looks to see why the cities were thus suffering from hardening of the arteries, one can detect significant changes in commerce and industry. During the first century the Augustan stabilization, together with the constant expansion of the frontiers, promoted an expanding economy. In the second century, after Hadrian's decision to abandon some of the Trajanic conquests, the frontiers remained static. Industry, as we have seen, tended to become more and more local, so reducing the potential volume of interprovincial trade. Technical progress of industry, which is relied upon today to increase markets and cut costs of production, was very slow in the ancient world, partly because of the existence of slavery, but more because of the divorce between science and industry and the relative insignificance of industry. Agriculture was always the main profession of ancient man, and the Romans paid much more attention to its improvement than to any other form of economic activity. The more interesting, then, is the fact that in the Empire agricultural science did not improve to any extent; if anything, it slipped backward in the shift from slaves to free sharecroppers.

By the second century the economy of the Empire began to slow, and then to halt, in its expansion. The budget of the state, however, far from changing in accordance, continued to increase as the imperial bureaucracy became more embracing and the imperial functions steadily grew in education, humanitarian activities, and frontier defense against the increasing barbarian pressure. Since state loans were rarely practicable in antiquity, the emperors had no choice but to squeeze ever greater sums out of an economy which was not expanding and in a society which did not like taxes. The results were slow inflation of the currency, forced supply of labor and material to the army, and a host of other devices to gain the needed funds. The conflict between the needs of the Empire and the limitations of its resources may have been an insoluble dilemma; certainly it appears such in the reply of Marcus Aurelius to his soldiers, when they demanded rewards after a victory. He doughtily refused, "declaring that whatever they obtained over and above the regular amount would be wrung from the blood of their parents and kinsmen." Marcus Aurelius had to spend most of his rule fighting on Rome's frontiers, and when he died in 180 the full brunt of the barbarian attacks was yet to come.

The Meaning of the Empire

Perhaps the most basic question which the "Roman peace" raises for a reflective student of history is this: Is materialism enough? The inhabitants of the Empire were generally prosperous in the first two centuries, yet the population stopped growing, perhaps even began to drop off before the end of the second century. Although the cities could afford great public works and monuments in profusion, the mighty Roman Empire produced less great art in two centuries than Athens poured out in three decades—nor would a comparison in literature, philosophy, or the drama redound any more to Rome's favor. More people could read than ever before in the world's history, but what masterpieces were the result?

Simply to pin the label of "materialism" on the Empire is, to be sure, to deal in the oversimple, for the Empire was a mass of contradictory trends and developments. Over against the many people who denied an afterlife by placing on their tombstones, "I am not, I was not, I don't care" (*non sum, non fui, non curo*), there were hosts who sought in Oriental religions some key to the meaning of life and death. But, taken by and large, the official tone of the Empire may justly be called one of emphasis on the material things of this life, and as such it was severely criticized by great sections of the populace. The Roman aristocrats, who wore themselves out in the idle luxury of the first century, had memories of a higher purpose in life, and in Seneca or Tacitus they vented their criticism of mere money-making. The satirists grew vitriolic on the subject; the Christians were more calmly scornful and perhaps more effective. By A.D. 180 new trends in thought were appearing in the Empire which marked an incipient swing away from materialism and the first beginnings of a break with the dominant lines of Graeco-Roman civilization. Not only in religion and philosophy but also in art and architecture one can see by the end of the second century that new life was somehow stirring which would lead to the entirely different concept of life in the Middle Ages. Further consideration of these developments must be left to the following essay.

Epilogue

IF ONE turns and looks back from A.D. 180 rather than forward, the story of Roman civilization appears as a fascinating segment of the development of western civilization. Beginning as a small city-state in central Italy, Rome early demonstrated its significant gifts by conquering all of Italy and at the same time reorganizing its internal system of government as a democracy. This dual process was complete by

270 B.C.; thus far Rome had had only intermittent contact with the eastern Mediterranean and its Greek-Hellenistic culture.

From 264 to approximately 133 B.C., as the Romans gained mastery over the eastern Mediterranean basin, the influence of Hellenistic culture became ever greater in the West. Both the ideas gained from the East and the wealth looted from the conquered countries led to trouble within the Roman social and political system, and the last century of the Republic was marked by bloody efforts to solve the problems raised by Rome's expansion.

Finally Augustus provided the answer which we know as the Principate or Empire, and Virgil stated the Roman purpose as one of bringing peace to the civilized world. The Augustan system did secure peace and prosperity for 200 years, during which ancient civilization could recover from the brutalities of the Roman conquest. The synthesis between Greek and Roman civilization already achieved in the first century B.C. was strengthened, and the resulting Mediterranean civilization was spread widely out from the central basin into the East, into Africa, and above all into central and western Europe as far as the Rhine and Scotland. This civilization, which we may describe as rational, naturalistic, urban, nonpolitical, and directed entirely toward life on this earth, was not markedly original; rather it accepted the works and ideas of the past and refashioned them in countless variations. The Middle Ages, it cannot be overemphasized, knew ancient culture almost entirely through the writings of these synthesizers of the Empire. In its system of government and law the purely Roman contribution looms the largest; in its sympathetic attitude toward man—humanitarianism—the Empire broke its freshest ground, as revealed in many pagans besides Seneca but above all in the body of Christian teaching and practice.

The significance in the general history of man of the "Roman peace" thus lies in two opposed but complementary aspects. First, it allowed a space in which ancient civilization could be pulled together and spread widely; and, secondly, it furnished a superb seedbed in which Christianity and other forces of the future might easily arise. Not to be forgotten, however, is the fact that the firm protection of the Empire allowed secure lives to generations of families living in Mediterranean lands.

To conclude this essay, we could do no better than to revert to Aelius Aristides, the Greek orator from Smyrna, with whom our story began. Aristides, it will be remembered, delivered a great oration in praise of Rome at the city itself in A.D. 144.

Today [he said] all the Greek cities arise again under your rule; . . . the sea coasts and interior districts abound in cities, either founded or enlarged by you and under your government. . . . As if summoned to a feast, all the civilized world has laid down the burden of its arms and has turned to decorate itself and to enjoy the delights of peace. . . . You have made the name of Rome no longer that of a city but of an entire people.

Rarely elsewhere in ancient authors can one find so keen an appreciation of the spirit of Roman government or so well-turned thanks for the prosperity which Rome had brought. That the inhabitants of this world also felt much as Aelius Aristides did is attested by the brief words carved again and again on inscriptions, expressing their gratitude to "the master of land and sea, the ruler of all the world."

Chronological Summary

B.C.

c.	5000	Invasion of Mediterranean-type people.
c.	2000	Beginning of Indo-European invasions.
c.	850	Arrival of Etruscans.
c.	800	Greek colonization in Sicily and South Italy.
c.	625	Union of Roman villages into city.
c.	500	Expulsion of Etruscan rulers of Rome; establishment of Republic.
	474	Syracuse and Cumae defeat Etruscans.
c.	466	Tribunate established.
c. 443–442		Twelve Tables.
	392	Fall of Veii.
	387	Invasion of Gauls; sack of Rome.
	334–323	Alexander's conquest; beginning of Hellenistic world.
	287	Struggle of patricians and plebeians ends.
	264–241	First Punic War.
	241	Livius Andronicus and first Roman plays.
	227	Organization of Sicily and of Sardinia and Corsica as provinces.
	218–201	Second Punic War.
	216	Battle of Cannae.
		Plautus, Naevius.
	200–196	War with Philip V of Macedon.

B.C.

	192–189	War with Antiochus III of Syria.
		Ennius; Terence; Cato the Censor; Scipio Aemilianus; Panaetius; Polybius.
	146	Destruction of Carthage.
	133	Reforms of Tiberius Gracchus; his murder.
	123–122	Reforms of Gaius Gracchus.
	102–101	Defeat of Cimbri and Teutons by Marius.
	90–88	Revolt of Italian allies; grant of citizenship to all Italy south of Po.

88–85   First Mithridatic War; Populares in control.
81–79   Dictatorship of Sulla; restoration of Senate.
70   Consulship of Pompey and Crassus.
        Lucretius; Catullus.
63   Consulship of Cicero; conspiracy of Catiline.
60   Formation of First Triumvirate.
59   Consulship of Caesar.
58–50   Caesar's conquest of Gaul.
49–44   Civil wars; Caesar's dictatorship.
44   Murder of Caesar.
43   Second Triumvirate; death of Cicero.
42   Battles of Philippi.
39–36   War of Octavian against Sextus Pompey.
32–31   War of Octavian against Antony.
30   Death of Antony and Cleopatra.

27 B.C.–A.D. 14
        Principate of Augustus.
        Livy, Virgil, Horace.
14–37   Tiberius.
37–41   Gaius (Caligula).
41–54   Claudius.
54–68   Nero.
        Seneca; Lucan.
68–69   Civil war.

A.D.
69–79   Vespasian.
79–81   Titus.
81–96   Domitian.
        Quintilian; Tacitus.
96–98   Nerva.
98–117 Trajan.
117–138 Hadrian.
138–161 Antoninus Pius.
161–180 Marcus Aurelius.

Suggestions for Further Reading~

GOOD one-volume histories of Rome are A. E. R. Boak, *History of Rome to 565 A.D.* (5th ed.; New York, 1965), and Max Cary, *History of Rome* (2d ed.; London, 1954). A three-volume political discussion is *History of the Roman World* (London, 1953–1961). The period 753–146 B.C. is treated by H. H. Scullard; 146–30 B.C., by F. B. Marsh; 30 B.C.–A.D. 138, by E. T. Salmon. For the Hellenistic world, see W. W. Tarn, *Hellenistic Civilisation* (New York, paperback 1961). The *Oxford Classical Dictionary* (Oxford, 1949), which has brief bibliographies, may be consulted on specific points. Fuller book lists may be found in the *Cambridge Ancient History*, Vols. VII–X (Cambridge, 1928–1934).

The classic history of the Roman Republic is Theodor Mommsen, *History of Rome* (Chicago, reprint 1957; abridged ed., New York, paperback 1958). Raymond Bloch, *Origins of Rome* (New York, 1960), sums up recent explorations; for Rome's early neighbors, see D. H. Lawrence, *Etruscan Places* (New York, paperback 1957); Massimo Pallottino, *Art of the Etruscans* (New York, 1955); B. H. Warmington, *Carthage* (Baltimore, paperback 1964). The Late Republic is discussed by F. R. Cowell, *Cicero and the Roman Republic* (Baltimore, paperback 1956); H. H. Scullard, *From the Gracchi to Nero* (New York, paperback 1959); and Ronald Syme, *Roman Revolution* (Oxford, paperback 1960).

In the Empire, Theodor Mommsen, *The Provinces of the Roman Empire* (New York, 1887), is a masterly interpretation of the light thrown by inscriptions on the prosperity of the provinces; Michael I. Rostovtzeff, *Social and Economic History of the Roman Empire* (2d ed.; Oxford, 1957), gives a thoughtful analysis of its development. Intellectual and other aspects may be found in Harold Mattingly, *Roman Imperial Civilization* (London, 1957); and Chester G. Starr, *Civilization and the Caesars* (Ithaca, 1954).

The following books on special topics in Roman culture and history are well written and generally interesting: Cyril Bailey, *The Legacy of Rome* (Oxford, 1923); Jerome Carcopino, *Daily Life in Ancient Rome* (New Haven, paperback 1960); Samuel Dill, *Roman Society from Nero to Marcus Aurelius* (New York, paperback 1956); J. Wight Duff, *Literary History of Rome from the Origins to the Close of the Golden Age* (rev. ed.; London, 1959) and *Literary History of Rome in the Silver Age* (rev. ed.; London, 1959); Leon P. Homo, *Roman Political Institutions* (New York, 1929); H. I. Marrou, *History of Education in Antiquity* (New York, paperback 1964); Harold Mattingly, *The Man in the Roman Street* (New York, 1947); H. J. Rose, *Ancient Roman Religion* (New York, paperback 1959); Fritz Schulz, *Principles of Roman Law* (Oxford, 1936).

For more information on Roman characters, read the brief but absorbing *Lives* by Plutarch (Modern Library and paperback editions). See also G. P. Baker, *Hannibal* (New York, 1929) and *Sulla the Fortunate* (New York, 1927); Gaston Boissier, *Cicero and His Friends* (New York, 1897); John Buchan, *Augustus* (Boston, 1937); M. P. Charlesworth, *Five Men: Character Studies from the Roman Empire* (Cambridge, Mass., 1936); Alfred Duggan, *King of Pontus* (New York, 1959), on Mithridates; W. Warde Fowler, *Julius Caesar* (New York, 1904); H. J. Haskell, *This Was Cicero* (New York, 1942); Hans Volkmann, *Cleopatra* (New York, 1958). One may learn a great deal also from rereading Shakespeare's *Julius Caesar*.

A deeper understanding of the Romans can be gained by reading their own literature. Horace, Livy, Petronius (*Satyricon*), Suetonius (gossipy *Lives* of the emperors), Tacitus, Virgil, and others are available in paperback in good translations.

Index